Cameo of Costume 1951 -1982

has kindly been sponsored by the following:
Diamond sponsors:Aeromark Ltd.

Donations
Mr & Mrs K. Brough
Mrs C. Davies
Mr & Mrs John Watson

Published by **Bugle Publications**
Tinkers Hoe, Queens Road, Colmworth, Bedford MK44 2LA

First published 2005

Copyright © Thelma L. Marks 2005

Illustrations:
Page 78 from a D'Arcy & Rosamunde Brochure
All other pen & ink drawings by Thelma Marks

Photographs:
from D'Arcy & Rosamunde advertising 1951-1982
and clientele

All rights reserved.
Without limiting the rights under copyright reserved above,
no part of this publication may be reproduced, in any form
or by any means (electronic, mechanical, photocoping,
recording or otherwise) without the prior written
permission of both the copyright owner and the
above publisher of this book.

Hardback ISBN 0-9551356-1-3

Cameo of Costume

1951   1982

The story of D'Arcy & Rosamunde of Bedford

by Thelma Marks

with a foreword by Caroline Bacon
Curator of the Cecil Higgins Art Gallery -Bedford

Foreword

On 12th November 2001, the Gallery held a very special afternoon soirée for the former staff of D'Arcy & Rosamunde, to celebrate the fiftieth anniversary of the formation of the business in Bedford and formally receive 56 bound volumes of the French fashion bible: "L'Officiel", which were used by them over the period between 1951 and 1982.

This reunion was to be the start of an extraordinary partnership between one of the firm's founders, Thelma Marks, and the Gallery. From the many reminiscences of the day and Thelma's very generous gift to the Gallery of examples of clothes made by D'Arcy & Rosamunde over the past fifty years, it became clear that an important piece of social history, not to mention Bedford's history, needed to be recorded for subsequent generations.

This is therefore the culmination of over two years of research and recall for Thelma, and the result is a fascinating insight into the post-war British fashion industry which I am sure will prove invaluable to the student and those who simply love clothes.

The Gallery is also honoured to have been given the D'Arcy & Rosamunde Archive to enable students to study fashion in Bedford. It is hoped that the superb array of clothes that have been donated by Thelma and her sister and partner Estelle Addington will be displayed in a purpose-built costume gallery within the decade.

Caroline Bacon
Curator, Cecil Higgins Art Gallery, Bedford
February 2004

This book is dedicated to my parents
Tom & Lily Eayrs
and all who worked at
D'Arcy & Rosamunde
between 1951 and 1982

This book would not have come to fruition without the encouragement of Caroline Bacon, the curator of the Cecil Higgins Art Gallery. Caroline wanted to know about the background of the D'Arcy & Rosamunde collection of clothes, which my sister Estelle Addington and I presented to the gallery. I am also indebted to my computer guru, Lynne Leonowicz, who has encouraged and helped me to get the project together. How fruitful has been the learning curve, and what fun it has been! So I should like to thank them both, along with my sister Estelle for her helpful comments, my friend Mary McKeown for proofreading and not least my husband David for his patience when buried in reminiscences and old records. I lost all sense of time!

Every effort has been made to contact those whose photographs appear in these pages. I should like to thank Mrs W Bushby and Mrs C Jefferson for their kind permission to reproduce the photographs on pages 39 and 43 respectively.

CONTENTS

	Foreword	*page 7*
1	*Haute Couture Comes to Bedford*	*page 11*
2	*Getting Going*	*page 23*
3	*The First Collection*	*page 27*
4	*Keeping Warm*	*page 31*
5	*More Customers*	*page 35*
6	*That Special Occasion*	*page 39*
7	*Next to Nellie*	*page 45*
8	*My Formative Years*	*page 49*
9	*The Business Grows*	*page 56*
10	*The End of an Era*	*page 66*
11	*The Swinging Sixties*	*page 69*
12	*Fashion Shows*	*page 74*
13	*Into the 1970s*	*page 85*
14	*Our 25th Anniversary*	*page 89*
15	*First Principles*	*page 93*
16	*The Easter Burglary*	*page 99*
17	*The Collection*	*page 102*
18	*Estelle's Footnote*	*page 107*
19	*Some Staff Comments*	*page 108*
20	*Some Statistics*	*page 110*
21	*The Practice of Couture*	*page 111*
22	*A Glossary of Terms*	*page 107*
23	*Inventory of Garments*	*page 123*
24	*Index*	*page 129*

1. Haute Couture comes to Bedford

"Who would want to go to the backwaters of Bedford?" I asked.

It was a dull and rainy Saturday at the end of November 1951 and my sister and I were home from London for the weekend. The suggestion came from my mother, who had heard that there was a business for sale in Harpur Street, Bedford, that might interest me. It all sounded pointless , as I was looking for some premises to start up a business in London. So far all that I had found within my budget was a basement in Grosvenor Square, but it had a large boiler in the middle of it! So I was working from our attic flat, at No 30 Cleveland Square, close to Lancaster Gate (if you were being kind with your description, but perhaps even closer to Paddington!). However, four flights of stairs would hardly entice customers, and the only telephone in the house was on the ground floor.

In 1946, just after the Second World War, London was an exciting place. I left school in Bedford to study fashion design at what is now the London College of Fashion, but then was called the Barrett Street Technical College. In spite of the name, it had always had a fine reputation and there was a good choice of jobs for students when they had completed their training. This was important for me, as my father had had a very lean time during the war, due to his farm being taken from him to make an emergency landing and training field for pilots. The " War Ag", as everyone called the War Agricultural Committee, had refused to return his farm to him at the end of the war, because they believed that they needed to plough up the

My father, as a handsome young soldier, aged twenty, just after he had been commissioned during the First World War.

grassland in order to grow more food. As a sheep and cattle farmer he did not have the machinery to plough up and cultivate his pastures .

A grant of £150 per year was awarded to me for two years of study. With this £3 a week, I was able to live in a hostel for 32s.6p per week, pay my train fare home from Kings Cross to St. Neots for just over 50 pence, and one penny per journey covered my bus fares around London. Lunch for five days was provided by a British Restaurant, which was a government initiative after the Blitz to provide cheap food for the worker in the cities, at the cost of two shillings and sixpence—equivalent to twelve and a half pence in today's money. It was pretty grotty, in the basement of a house, and the food was a simple fare of mince in various forms with apple tart to follow. With this modest expenditure, I was left with sufficient change to occasionally queue for the gods at the opera or theatre, or go to the "Pictures".

The wages of £3.10s at my first job gave me ten shillings (fifty pence) extra, and I was able to consider joining three other girls to share a flat. I could have earned a lot more if I had gone into "wholesale" but at that time I wanted to work for a theatrical costumier. It was a great experience but very hard work, and I learnt a lot about life. Sufficient, in fact, to decide that it was not the life for me! Back at college, another job was found for me, working in PR under the artist Francis Madden, designing and producing display material for a well-known wholesale company. This was much more fun and, although I worked for the firm, I was my own boss, as I could arrange my own work schedules for the whole season. This I did for two seasons until the company invited me to design half a dozen models for their

All of my designs bore a D'Arcy label, the name which I registered, when I first decided to start up in business on my own in London in 1951.

summer collection, giving me the leftover, written-down fabrics in stock from the previous season that needed to be cleared. I was thrilled to have the opportunity, but it made me very unpopular for a number of reasons. The two young assistant designers resented me because I had my own silk-screening studio up on the top floor of the building. I then blotted my copybook with the two older designers, by producing the winner of the season. New fabric had to be found in order to complete the orders, and by the next season the senior designer made sure to sabotage all of my designs in order to prevent it from happening again. This made life very frustrating, so it was obviously time for a change. Perhaps it was better to be an artist after all, I thought.

Since leaving college I had been attending classes at St. Martin's College of Art, in Charing Cross Road, which had increased my confidence, but, I thought, perhaps I should dress the part before applying for another job. So I bought a beret and made a pussycat bow to wear with my dark red swing coat. Applying for my first job as an artist I arrived to find six men, all with very large black folders, waiting to be interviewed. They all looked very professional, so I didn't hold out much hope of success. However, to my surprise, probably because I was female and thus lower paid, I was offered the job. I was to be personal assistant to the designer of display stands working for a subsidiary of the fifth largest timber company in the country. Our raw material was all the off-cuts, from which we designed display stands for the motor and cosmetics industry and for Olympia. This was a fascinating experience, which I would not have missed.

The company was in Hanwell, Middlesex, and I

lived in the West End of London. This resulted in having to catch an empty train out in the morning and return in an empty train in the evening. As I watched the packed commuter trains going in the opposite direction, I resolved never to be caught in those uncomfortable circumstances when it was possible to do otherwise. This experience was probably one of the greatest influences of my life, for I have tended to do the opposite of most people and refused to follow any "fashion" slavishly.

Anyone who can design and make clothes is never without a job. There is always someone who wants something special for an occasion, and I continued to design and make garments in the evenings. Eventually, after about eighteen months, I was persuaded that I was wasting my talents and should start up in business on my own. I had sufficient customers to keep body and soul together, so I took the plunge. In the meantime, my sister Estelle had joined me in the flat and became a trainee for a year at Dickins and Jones. She used her entrepreneurial skills to increase our housekeeping budget by auctioning some of our rations in the staff room, particularly bacon, which we did not like. When she arrived in London she looked like a young colt and was really more interested in being a young farmer than anything else. However, a course at the Cherry Marshall Model Agency changed her appearance and she soon emerged as a beautiful model, tall and elegant, with her long hair coiffured into a bun. She immediately got a job with a well-known wholesale house where she worked, until one day one of the directors told her that he was taking her to Scotland for the weekend, with the Collection! Using her sixth sense, she declined to go, and was promptly sacked. So by that November day in

Some of my early designs.
The dress, made of striped patterned fabric, shows the stripes falling down to a mitre at the back, which was one of my favourite slimming devices. I believed that horizontal stripes were more flattering than vertical stripes, which just served to outline the shape!

14

A jade green wool barathea suit with cuffs of sable fur, had a double breasted jacket with a low narrow square neckline. A matching sash was tied over the shoulder.

1951, neither of us was gainfully employed in the strict sense of the word, and doubtless both our parents were rather worried about us in the big city!

Now, the rain continued to pour throughout our drive to Bedford and was still tipping it down on our arrival. We parked diagonally in the centre of Harpur Street opposite the lingerie shop, Gladys Clayton. The window was sparsely displayed with expensive lingerie, and next door at the music shop, Frasers, the sound of a piano could be heard. We called in at the little children's shop, where our school clothes had been purchased, to see Jessie Jackson. What a kind soul she had been to all the children. They knew that if they lost their fare home, they could always call in at her shop to borrow it. Many of them passed by as they walked down the little side street to the bus station behind, in the Broadway.

Jessie had told my mother about this shop called Rosamunde. During the war it had been very successful with a good reputation, having been kept by two sisters, Mrs Douglas and Mrs Ross. After the war they had retired to Devon and the shop had been bought by a lady who had been a book-keeper at Hockliffe's, the stationers. She thought that she had a flair for fashion, but had no concept of what was entailed. As a result she had found herself deeply in debt and had put the business up for sale.

The rain continued to fall as we made a dash across the road and up the steps of Rosamunde. It was dark and dingy, just one small room painted in cream, with clothes hanging limply on metal bar stands. A large lady, with long beads hanging over her ample bosom, sniffed at us. She was not at all my idea of a "vendeuse", but she obviously realised that we were not customers. We asked to see the owner. When she came, she was small and mouse-like. I wondered how she stood up to the large lady!

Mrs May opened the tightly packed cupboards to show us the stock. The first impression was of drab colours: maroons and beige, cream and navy. There were tweeds skirts and suits with so many colours mixed in them that they looked, at a distance, the colour of mud. Other suits were made of heavy ribbed jersey or what looked like a loosely crocheted wool, from a firm called Lafega, whose fabric was made by the blind. Later we learnt that these suits were highly prized by the old ladies, but to us, they just seemed dull, over-priced garments. Some time had passed since the lifting of restrictions imposed by the wartime "utility" rules, but some garments still bore that label. I shuddered as I realised that some of the cupboards were too narrow for the clothes and were damaging their sleeves. So the styles were only suitable for old people, except for some ghastly slinky dresses of gold lurex, which were quite without taste. This type of business was certainly not for me!

"Perhaps you would like to see the workroom now," she said. So we were taken along the dark, back hallway of the early Victorian house, out across a small gravelled courtyard to a single-storey brick building, with skylights in the roof. As she put the lights on, we saw a small office which led into a brightly lit workroom. It had probably been built in the 1930s, had a polished parquet floor and grilles at the south-facing windows. My eyes opened even wider as she proceeded to show us the wages book and tell us about the girls who

Miss Clara Faulkner

worked there. Here was a gem of a workroom, with the statutory wages in Bedford almost half those payable in London! But I had no money except my small savings and could not find the wages, let alone buy the business, so we thanked her and returned home. I was in a sad and reflective mood. I sat quietly in the back of the car and said nothing.

At supper time my father asked what we had been doing during the day. I told him of our experiences and said that, of course, it was an impossible dream. "Would you really like it?" he asked. "Yes, but it is not possible," I said. So he told me that he had just sold his first crop from his newly returned farm and could find the necessary money, if it was a reasonable and practical proposition. So he telephoned a friend, who was an auctioneer, to ask for his opinion, and it was arranged that we should all go to Bedford early in the week to look into it further.

This time it was not raining, and I began to see the possibilities of the shop. The stock still looked just as dreary as before and the large sales lady was no more affable than on our Saturday visit. This time, however, the staff were in the workroom. Sitting in the middle on a very high chair, with her feet resting on the cover of a sewing machine, was Miss Faulkner, the tailoress, who, I was told, had been trained at Beagleys (the men's outfitters & tailors) in Bedford. As she greeted me, I noted that she had iron-grey hair and dark eyes; and I returned her greeting with great respect, as, having attended a tailoring course for one year under a Savile Row tailor, I knew that it took at least fifteen years to acquire this skill. Seated opposite each other at a table were two senior girls, Margaret and Sylvia, and each had a junior sitting alongside her, whom she was training. This form of apprenticeship, the "Next to Nellie" system, was very good, provided that "Nellie" was prepared to give the time and attention necessary for the training of the apprentice.

Looking to the end of the room, I saw a large ironing table, with a row of gas rings standing behind the table. On each ring stood a different size of flat-iron waiting to be used. There was electricity, because there were two electric fires burning (the two bar variety), but it seemed very cold. I think that the irons were as much for warming as ironing, but it seemed very archaic for 1951. Later, a lady who kept an antique shop in St. Peter's told me that she would wrap herself in brown paper and iron herself to get warm at night, never taking off her clothes and sleeping in a chair; so maybe that is how they kept warm!

The deal was done: £2,000 for the stock, £2,000 for the goodwill and £1,000 for the fixtures and fittings. The last figure was laughable, for the lot needed binning, but Mrs. May stood firm and those were her terms. On the 8th December 1951 we took over the shop and immediately painted the showroom a pale apple green. The back room, previously used as an inner sanctum for favoured customers, was opened up by removing the double doors dividing the two rooms. All the curtains were taken down and sent to the cleaners, where they were dyed a royal shade of purple. These were used to create changing-room cubicles in the alcoves of the chimney breasts. A friend gave us a beautiful antique gilt mirror that filled the wall by the entrance. I had found an elegant Regency card table, sadly without a top. However, once fitted with a mirror instead, it reflected the bouquet of flowers that was placed on the surface. In this way a completely new impression was created,

There was a row of gas rings each of which had a flat-iron on it, ready for ironing. Under the table was a bucket of water to wring out a cloth, which was then used to clean the bottom of the iron and reduce it to the required temperature. This operation created much sizzling and steam as the iron was banged onto the folded wet cloth......

These two irons weighed 10lbs and 14lbs respectively. They were made by J & J Siddons of West Bromwich.

It was necessary to have a really strong wrist to handle these irons which were used in tailoring, mostly by men.

Today, they are equally valuable for flattening my watercolour paper !

and became an important part of our elegant new look.

We did not employ the large lady. She did not like changes and she did not like us, just two young girls, aged eighteen and twenty-one. We were not alone, however, as we were ably supported by my mother. I had expected the business to be bought in her name, or at least that she would be a partner, but my father had said a firm "no," because he felt it was wrong to mix the generations. He said that Estelle and I must stand or fall on our own merit, and in retrospect it was a very wise move. This was the result of his own experiences and, predictably, his father thought that he was mad. "Those girls will just lose all of your money," he was told.

The Westminster Bank manager had not agreed with his ideas of setting up in business either. "How much capital are you going to give your daughters to run this business?" he asked. "Capital!" my father exploded. "They have two thousand pounds worth of stock, they must sell that for their capital." But the manager did not agree, and would not open an account without a reasonable amount of capital to run the business. So we had walked along the High Street to Lloyds Bank, whose manager understood my father's sentiments better. He agreed to open an account, provided that my father would give a guarantee on it. In the event, our wages bills were paid for us for six weeks, and we never had the occasion to borrow any money again, although it was a close call on many occasions. Metaphorically, we had always been taught to cut our garments according to how much cloth we had, and it worked well in practice. We ran frugal lives, living at home for free and taking out the minimum in cash of

£3 a week each, in order to accrue capital. In this way we were able to accumulate cash so that the business could grow.

There was great excitement when our first real customer arrived. Tall and haughty, she swept into the showroom. I suppose that you might describe her as a "county" customer. She ordered two expensive suits and the order was dispatched. In due course the suits arrived and we telephoned the customer to let her know that the suits were here. To our horror, she tried them both on and then announced that she did not like either of them! Knowing that we were depending on her payment to settle our bill with the wholesaler, I pulled myself up to my full five feet four inches and said: "I am afraid that you ordered both of these suits and, whilst it is possible to make one mistake, you cannot have made two mistakes, so I must insist that you take at least one of them." If there had been money in the bank to pay for them, I doubt I would have had the audacity to challenge her, but, though she grumbled, she did pay for one of them. Thus we had cleared our first hurdle; for the custom was to put 100% mark-up on to garments and this early lesson justified it. The sale of the one suit generated just enough to pay our bill to the manufacturer.

Our first impression was that it was highway robbery to put such a large mark-up on to stock. However we soon learnt from our accountant that when the rent, rates, electricity, wages and all the other overheads and incidentals were paid, the profit might be only five or ten per cent. Most people who are not involved in business do not understand the difference between **mark-up** and **profit**, so this was an early lesson. Estelle was a wizard with figures and rapidly got to grips

My father, Tom Eayrs, as I sketched him later in life, —in repose. He did not enjoy good health, as he had been through the Battle of the Somme in the first World War, —only to be injured seriously just ten days before Armistice.

with the book-keeping and stock-taking, and generally kept tabs on what was being spent. The books had to balance to the last penny, even the petty cash. Without Estelle, there would not have been a business, because I find it very difficult to concentrate on other things AND think about the money side as well. So balancing the books was her main speciality, although she was a super sales person too. All of the old ladies loved her, because she was kind and had a good sense of fun. And since she was also tall and beautiful, those with eligible sons would find some excuse to get them into the shop to meet her. As a result, we managed to get some free electrical advice and other help.

Business was very slow at the beginning. Another "county" lady arrived to have a suit made and, when it was completed, I asked: "Will it be cash or cheque, madame?", which was the prescribed way to present the bill. She nearly exploded with indignation. "I never pay for one suit until I am ready to order the next one," she said, to which Estelle replied: "I am very sorry but we have to pay our bills and the price quoted is for cash payment. If you require credit, the price will have to be increased!" Whereupon the customer paid up immediately but grumbled, as she left the shop, "I've never paid my tailor or dressmaker like this before." As a result of this tough policy, we never acquired bad debts, and our accountant wanted to know how we achieved it!

Meeting and getting to know the customers was the continuation of our education. We had a wonderful mentor in "Matty." His real name was Ettrick Napier Mathieson and he came into our lives in 1945. Having arrived in St. Neots late one night after being demobbed from the

Ettrick Napier Mathieson, sketched in 1956

army, he went to the police station, as the hotel room that he had booked had not been kept for him and there was nowhere for him to stay. My father, on duty as a Special Constable said: "You can come home with me. The maid's room is not used and I can soon make you up a bed, as the family are away on holiday." Matty was very grateful and asked my mother, on her return, if he could stay for a few days longer until he found some accommodation locally. He got on very well with all the family and the few days extended to a fortnight, and finally to twenty-five years! He was in business, and guided us in writing our early business letters, taking account of the legal position with regards to the written word. He advised us never to apologise if something went wrong, as is inevitable sometimes, but always to "sincerely regret" a situation. My father was full of earthy good sense, but Matty was always there for us with his business experience and we benefited from his mistakes, which he did not hide.

The Eastern Electricity Board deliver their first storage heaters in Bedford to D'Arcy and Rosamunde at No 42 Harpur Street.

2. Getting Going

The workroom was the hub of the activity for the business at the beginning, but it was not a very hospitable place in which to work. It was hot during the summer and very cold during the winter. Maybe the heavily barred windows had been installed because of the close proximity of the prison, whose high wall was on the opposite side of the back road. Along with the parquet floors, which shone and gave a feeling of the utmost modernity, it all seemed rather bleak and felt a bit like a prison. The separation of the buildings was also not the most convenient arrangement in all weathers, for, apart from the draughts, the landlady who lived above had a habit of coming downstairs and bolting the door on us! One of our early changes involved buying some electric irons and installing storage heaters. We were in fact the first business in Bedford to install this new form of heating, and the electricity company took the photograph of them arriving, for publicity in the local paper. The storage heaters gave background heat, but it seemed warm if the temperature rose to 60°F.

Right from the start, the workroom was busy all the time, but, having taken over the business at the end of a very bad season, we had some days when we did not see a customer in the showroom. At times, my mother and my sister would be reduced to playing canasta to pass the time until we got on stream for our first show.

Clearly, since we had no money to buy any stock, we had to assess and sell the clothes that were in the showroom. Once these had been pressed and

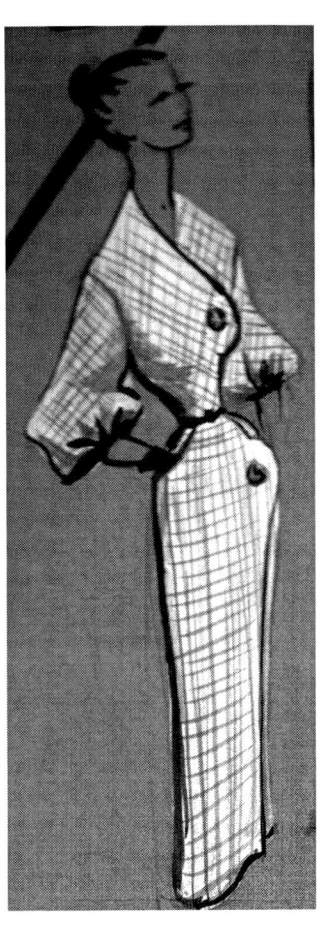

This fine wool suiting dress was designed for my sister, Estelle. It was made in a pale grey dog-tooth check and she wore it in the showroom in 1953.

The new electric night storage heaters (one can be seen on the right of the picture, behind the sewing machine) are installed in the workroom.

repaired we held a SALE. One dark red Lafega suit was reduced from 35 guineas to £4, much to the delight of the old lady who bought it. "I never expected to be able to afford a Lafega suit," she said and would give us a big smile every time she went by the shop wearing the suit. Little did she know that Miss Faulkner had invisibly darned forty-two moth holes in it before it was put into the window for sale! Most of the clothes were priced in guineas, a guinea being worth £1 and 1 shilling. It was a custom from the past used by high-class establishments, although guineas were no longer in circulation.

There were very few orders on the books, just the odd skirt or two to make. It was clear that we could not carry the two apprentices, who seemed to be kept for tea-making, sweeping the workroom, shopping, making shoulder clips and cleaning the pins collected from the floor.

So one of my first unpleasant duties was to explain the situation to them and give them notice. However, one of them was subsequently re-employed as soon as the situation improved. After the first six weeks' wages had been paid by my father, we were independent. Thereafter he had his suits tailored in the workroom by Miss Faulkner from Hardy's "thorn proof" tweeds as a form of interest on his investment! At last he had found a tailor whose suits fitted him. Previously, his jackets were never cut wide enough across the back, but I soon found out the reason for his problem. Having been in the army, whenever he went to be measured he would pull back his shoulders in a parade-ground stance! Thus when the suit was made he was unable to relax forward in a natural position and complained that the suit had been cut too narrow across the back. So, once his problem was realised, I was able to allow lots of width across the back and fit him generously. My father would attend our subsequent dress shows with a big smile on his face, wearing his new suit. Seeing the result of his investment also gave him enormous pleasure and satisfaction.

D'Arcy & Rosamunde showrooms on the right, with the hat & shoe showroom on the left. Our shoes came on a franchise from the Northampton-based "Bodileys".

The fabric of the evening gown was woven into wide black velvet stripes with narrower bright yellow ruched taffeta stripes - giving it the effect of a wasp!

Opposite page: the back view.

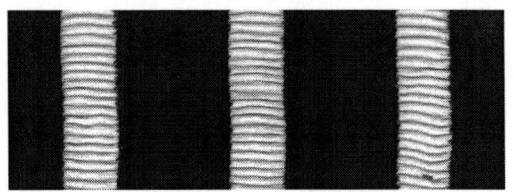

3. The First Collection

This was the opportunity for which I had been waiting, and I immediately began to prepare my first collection for the Spring of 1952, with Estelle as the principal model. In the meantime, I worked night and day to get the workroom going. A few orders had been brought with me, notably a second embroidered velvet suit and cloak for the eccentric head of Cedar House School at St. Neots. She was kind and charming, and I got on well with her, but could not appreciate her taste in dress. The first suit was a deep turquoise velvet and the second one a royal purple. The jackets were made with a scalloped hem, lined with a contrasting pure silk chiffon, with embroidery on the pockets and lapels. The skirts had sixteen cross-cut gores in them, with a scalloped hem to match! When business improved, I declined to make any more of these suits, making the excuse that the embroideress had gone to Australia, which was true. However, she continued as a customer, having less exotic clothes made.

Soon after we opened, a very smart lady arrived and ordered two beautiful and costly dresses to be made. I was thrilled, as this was as a result of seeing the purple and turquoise striped strapless dress that I had been wearing at the local balls. So the evening gown that was designed for her was in yellow ruched silk and black velvet stripes, which she called her wasp dress. It was as a result of the experience gained with Joy Ricardo, the theatrical designer, that I was able to make well fitted strapless dresses. In fact a corselette was made for every customer to ensure a good shape before any dress was designed. As a result, we acquired a regular customer who shopped each season for the next thirty-one years, and became one of our prime advertisements.

Whilst the stock was being sorted out, I scoured the stores for remnants with character, and bought a few lengths of quality fabrics, setting up accounts where possible. Estelle and I decided to lash out and buy one or two ready-to-wear suits from my favourite manufacturer, Simon Massey in Grosvenor Street. When we went in to introduce ourselves to the owner, Jack Freedman, he thought that we were models applying for a job! Once we explained our position, he was extremely kind and only allowed us to buy four suits. "Come back next week when you have sold them," he said, "And then you can buy some more." He became one of our trusted advisors and was an enormous help. He sent us to the well known fabric firm of Jacqmar in Grosvenor Street, where Pauline looked after us by finding fantastic remnants of original fabrics to get us going. It was a long and happy arrangement. The accountant at Jacqmar advised us to consult the Customs and Excise to simplify matters with regards to the paying of purchase tax. At eighteen and twenty-one years old, we were very green at the time!

Business was slowly picking up, so we were able to visit our next wholesaler, also in Grosvenor Street, called Rima. Here we were greeted by a waiter in tails giving out champagne. "Oh dear, we must be careful," I thought, as we had little to spend! In the event, we bought some very pretty summer dresses from their inexpensive range – "Atrima", which were bright inexpensive cotton dresses and just right for the coming show.

D'ARCY & ROSAMUNDE
present their
Spring Collection
March 1952

1   D'Arcy - THE TEMPEST
2   D'Arcy - MEASURE FOR MEASURE
3   Matita - Daybreak
4   D'Arcy - A WINTER'S TALE
5   Stolas - Country Club
6   Stolas - Grouse
7   D'Arcy - ROMEO
8   Stolas - Cricket
9   D'Arcy - HAMLET
10 Matita - Chequers
11. Biscuit
12 Shulamite
13 Cadet
14. Firefly
15 Apres Midi
16 Simon Massey - Esplanade
17 Simon Massey - Pedalo
18 Zamet - Globetrotter
19 Simon Massey - Lancer
20 Zamet - Portland
21 Simon Massey - Bubble
22 Matita - Portia
23 D'Arcy - LADY GREY
24 Atrima - Sweet Seventeen
25 Atrima - Olivia
26 Aberdeen
27 Atrima - Pleiades

28 - 35 *Millinery Interval*

36 D'Arcy - CYMBELINE
37 Bel Robe - Penny Plain
38 Atrima - Sand
39 Zamet - D'Asta
40 D'Arcy - TWELFTH NIGHT
41 Bel Robe - Golden Hour
42 D'Arcy - JULIET
43 D'Arcy -CLEOPATRA
44 D'Arcy - MELROSE
45 D'Arcy - TURTLE DOVE
46 D'Arcy - TITANIA
47 D'Arcy - MUCH ADO ABOUT NOTHING
48 D'Arcy - WHAT YOU WILL
49 MIDSUMMER NIGHT'S DREAM
50 ALL'S WELL THAT ENDS WELL

42 HARPUR STREET, BEDFORD
Telephone: BEDFORD 2157

These are typical of cotton dresses that we bought from Atrima. Horizontal stripes were very popular at that time, with many similar ones being produced by Horrocks. The dresses shown here were made of the famous Marcel Boussac cotton.

As a designer, I was anxious to get started on the show. Sixteen outfits were designed, in order to demonstrate the range of our ability. Estelle had a wardrobe of clothes designed for her, as she was our best advertisement. There was a sea-green suit in fine wool barathea, the sleeves trimmed with sable cuffs. This was to show the excellence of Miss Faulkner's tailoring. There was a dark grey mohair coat with lots of swing to it and enormous buttons, worn over a grey and white striped wool dress. The stripes were cut horizontally, with an all-round pleated skirt, set on a low hipline. The bodice had a sailor collar, and again the dress had lots of swing about it. There was saucy beachwear which we included as something outrageous that we did not expect to sell, but just to cause a commotion or a laugh. The show was held at the beginning of March in the showroom. Some chairs were kindly loaned to us by the Convent, where we had previously been at school. I compèred the show. Our landlady allowed Estelle and the other two models to use the hallway for dressing, and she and her daughter attended the show.

In order to help with the expenses, we invited the lady from the hat shop next door to show her hats. This worked tolerably well, but she provided her own model, who looked wonderful in hats but was rather difficult to fit up with clothes. So we ended up with a millinery interlude in the middle of the show, all shown with a neutral, black or navy outfit.

Most of our outfits were named after Shakespeare's characters or plays. My heart soared when one of the customers stood up and applauded at the end. It was particularly gratifying, as she had connections in the fashion industry and could have afforded to shop anywhere. Subsequently she became a long-standing but very demanding customer, though I could always forgive her anything because of that visible early encouragement.

There were lots of lesson to learn. Even though most of the people with money were older folk, we could not rid ourselves quickly enough of the elderly-looking clothes. Fortunately the styles did not alter much, so it was difficult to tell how long a garment had been in stock. It soon became apparent to us that a young person with a good figure could look beautiful in anything, but to transform someone with a difficult figure gave you a customer for life. So in spite of our youth, this aspect of the business was a a great challenge. Right from the start, we had enthusiastic support from my mother. She was a good-looking elegant woman, who would never have worn the fuddy-duddy clothes that we inherited with the business. So in dressing her, we had an example of how an older woman could look, without appearing to be mutton dressed up as lamb, which at that time was an important cultural consideration.

Lily Eayrs (née Hull)
of Church Farm Roxton,
the mother of Thelma and Estelle, who supported her two daughters in a multitude of ways from selling to modelling, babysitting to cooking! Being a local girl, she was very well known in the area, which obviously helped when we were starting the business. This picture was taken when she was eighty-five , in 1990.

4. Keeping Warm

The feel of the magnificent Mink

Since time immemorial, man has worn fur to keep warm in winter. So learning about furs was a logical progression for me in the fashion trade. In the beginning I did not like furs at all. I could never afford one, and anyone that I knew who wore one—such as one of my aunts—only possessed a mangy "antique" specimen. Generally, furs were for the rich and were considered a status symbol. So it was not until I was prevailed upon to try one on, that I realized their seductive power! Trevor Fenwick, the furrier in Bedford, called shortly after we had arrived in Bedford, to introduce himself, for as he said: "We have complementary businesses." Finding out that neither Estelle nor I had any knowledge of furs, he then set about educating us in their merits. Trevor's elegant showroom was on the first floor in one of the early Victorian terrace houses on the south side of Goldington Road beyond St Peter's Street. Everything was cream and minimal in order to avoid detracting from the beauty of the furs. On our arrival, he produced fur after fur and told us of their special merits. They were shown with pride and loving care. Sable and ermine topped his list. All of the best furs came from Siberia or Northern Canada, where the extreme cold produced animals with the thickest fur and toughest skins. Traditionally sables and ermine were used by the nobility for trimming their Court gowns for special occasions.

Then came mink , the fur of the film stars. Natural wild mink was the most desirable, but the mink, being a crafty animal, rarely got caught and so the price was high. The most common mink was the Farmed Mink. Again, the best coats were natural ones, but the less attractive skins were dyed to more pleasing shades of black, brown or grey. However, its main disadvantage was that it marked badly. So it was necessary to be continually shaking it, in order to restore its smooth look. Eventually the dyed minks tended to fade, and not always to an attractive shade. Squirrel followed mink and was not nearly so expensive. Long coats moved beautifully and rippled when moving. It was a very soft fur, which was stranded and stitched to look like mink. My first purchase of fur was the tiny shoulder stole that was bought for warmth and not prestige for about £25, to wear at the balls.

Every Friday from October to March during the late 1940s and early 1950s, there was a **Ball.** They were organised by the Bachelors, the Farmers, the Young Farmers, the Rugby Club, the Tennis Club. the Squash Club and many others, not forgetting the Hunt and the Beagles. These balls were held in large country houses and in the Corn Exchange or Public Rooms, none of which had any heating at that time, except perhaps for a huge fire in the ball room at Kimbolton Castle or Hinchingbrook Castle. Both of these elegant mansions were still in the hands of their gentry owners, who had been unable to spend money or find the materials for restoration, even if they could have afforded to do so, as was the case with all of the public buildings. All of these venues were cold, draughty and dusty -- so much so that when dancing in a full length, full-skirted dress, one became a human vacuum cleaner. Thus I would arrive home with legs that were dirty to the knicker line and must have a strip wash before going to bed. None of the original tiered slips survived and the dresses of the period are quite grubby. The little shoulder fur was a

Thelma in the striking purple and turquoise striped taffeta strapless evening gown, which caused so much comment at the post-war balls in 1948.

great comfort as it could be worn all evening, even for dancing if your partners were not energetic enough to keep you warm! The smoochy type was definitely not welcomed...

The country-woman's fur was the musquash. Sometimes a heavyweight skin but at other times quite soft, this fur was hard-wearing and not costly. In fifty years I have had two natural pale musquash jackets, which proved light, warm and very comfortable. Again, this skin was mostly dyed and often stranded and seamed to look more streamlined. For the more sporty type, sheepskin jackets were almost a uniform at the races. They were more practical to wear in the wind and rain, for the wool is on the inside and the outside pelt is waterproof. Furs, on the other hand, look very sad when they get wet! There were other, more practical furs available, such as ponyskin or astrakhan, a lambskin with a curled wool from the Middle East. This latter skin was the first one to be imitated in fabric. Beaver and sealskin were glossy and plain, rather like a bearskin but with shorter hairs. The skin that I disliked most was the fox. Coats were occasionally made from them but conjured up the image of a lady of the streets. More usually, the whole skin of the animal, along with its head, was made into a stole that smart women would drape around their necks during the Twenties and Thirties. Thankfully, by the time that we had arrived on the fashion scene, this was no longer in vogue, but that didn't prevent a stream of ladies asking if we had any ideas for renovating them.

In the summer, furs were taken to the furrier to be put into cold storage. This was necessary, along with oiling and greasing, in order to prevent them drying out and to keep the skins supple and glossy.

Left in the warmth, the dried skins became like paper—tearing at the points of strain i.e. across the shoulders and around the armholes. Fur coats that had not received appropriate care became worn and mangy looking and could often be found in the charity shops, as they became fashionable for the young in the Sixties and Seventies. By the 1980s, the Animal Rights organisation had become so strident that it was unsafe to walk around London in any sort of fur. Women walking out of Harrods in fur coats risked having paint or raw eggs thrown at them.

Certainly the World Wide Fund for Nature brought to the attention of the public the cruelty to which some wild animals were subjected, along with the fact that many were being hunted out of existence. This was imperative, as the leopard, ocelot and lynx had been almost unobtainable since the 1950s. As a result, Trevor Fenwick bought from the wholesalers all the waste skins from the ocelot paws, collected over many years, which were usually thrown away or kept for repairing coats. He then designed and made two jackets, one of which I purchased as a rarity. It was a very special coat for me and I loved wearing it. Warm and sporty looking, it was worn when travelling to the Alps to ski, as rarely was there much heating in trains at that time and air travel had not yet become popular for travelling to ski resorts. Apart from the two coats made by Trevor, I have never seen another one like it. Finally there was rabbit or marmot, but those furs did not feature in Trevor's collection! You could buy those at E.P. Rose and Sons, for a song. If, however, you could not afford the luxury of a fur to keep you warm, winter clothes generally were made out of much warmer and heavier fabrics at that time when there was no universal central heating.

CORONATION 1953

5. More Customers

> One Monday morning the window was being dressed and a plaster model was temporarily without any clothes. A chauffeur-driven customer entered the showroom with the anguished plea: **"Please get that model covered immediately, as my chauffeur is sitting outside and will see it!"** *Technically, we should have covered the models with sheets immediately as the clothes were removed...*

A very smart and demanding customer from Wellingborough, who had most of her clothes designed and made by us, arrived one day in great consternation. Her tailor had just committed suicide by putting his head in the gas oven *and* she was the last person to see him alive! Fortunately, having had the benefit of a very good training, I was confident in **my** skills, but there were some customers who would test even a saint. I envied my sister's height, which helped in these situations. Another customer brought in a Paris original gown which she wanted me to copy in three different materials. Once the dresses were completed, she stripped to the "altogether", and put on her dress and then each of the three new dresses, one by one on top of the original model, to make sure that all the seams were in exactly the same place. The exertion taxed her too much; she almost swooned and demanded brandy, in spite of all of the dresses passing her stringent test.

Not all the customers were "county" folk. Some of the biggest spenders were the fair folk, who came in with wads of cash and wanted only the best. In fact, we often did not have clothes which were expensive enough for them, or with big enough fur collars on the coats (their favourites presumably because it was cold standing on a fairground). So they would say: "Oh dear, we'll 'ave to go to 'arrods now." But as we got to know them, they proved to be lovely people and were regular customers when in town. There were other tradespeople who took a lot of cash. They spent it with careless abandon and great joy. Training them to spend their hard-earned cash in a practical way was a challenge. Telling people *not* to spend money that day, but to come back in two weeks when there would be something better suiting their needs, was difficult. If you succeeded, then you won loyalty, as they appreciated the benefits of planning a wardrobe, whilst others resented any interference or suggestions at all. Then you would hope that they didn't tell anyone where they bought their clothes! One curvaceous American customer would be fitted up with the right size and then say: "Yes, it fits but I'll take the size smaller, please." And there was the elderly customer, who dyed her hair blonde and continued to wear the waspy-waisted corset of her youth. She constantly dressed in fluffy pale pink, long before Barbara Cartland espoused the fashion.

When training showroom staff, one of our cardinal rules was that however anyone looked, they were to be treated exactly the same, with respect. On one occasion an elderly gentleman came in to the shop and asked if we could fit his wife out for her to go to Buckingham Palace. He explained that she was in poor health and had broken her arm. It was touching when he brought her in. How kindly he looked after her, for she was clearly incontinent and not very clean. I coped and managed to fit her out, gasping for air at intervals. When he wrote the cheque I was amazed to find that he was titled and one of our foremost and best known admirals of the Second World War.

On another occasion two ladies arrived just around midday, looking for an outfit to wear at Ascot Races, during the following week. I showed them a D'Arcy outfit, made for that season's show. It had almost been sold the previous week to a lady for the same occasion, but she decided that she

A typical D'Arcy & Rosamunde window display, showing " Mini Brides " - for all our brides' gowns were individually designed and made to order.

could not afford it. It was a full-length duster coat over a matching sheath dress, made of heavy pure silk white grosgrain, overprinted with a nutmeg-brown paisley design. It almost fitted one of the ladies, and she fell in love with it. Could it possibly be altered whilst she had lunch in the town, as she was only passing through on her way home to Wimbledon? A rapid fitting ensued, as one of the girls agreed to change her lunch-hour. The bill was made out and it was sold to a Mrs Graham. At the end of the following week, the original customer who had nearly bought the outfit came into the showroom. She was most annoyed. How dare we tell her that the outfit that she had so nearly bought was an original D'Arcy Model. She had seen Elizabeth Arden lead in her winning horse in an *identical* outfit at Ascot only this week! We explained that the outfit had been sold to a Mrs Graham, and all was forgiven, when it was realised that Mrs Graham was indeed the real name of Elizabeth Arden.

Probably our most outrageous customer was a small blonde bombshell who thought that she could outwit gravity. She brought to us some grey lace to be made into an evening gown. "No," she said, "I will not have it boned, for if it is fitted properly, I have a sufficiently curvaceous figure to hold the dress up." So a very close-fitting, slinky fish-tailed dress was made and she took delivery of it. A few days later she returned with the lace dress, in high dudgeon. To our amazement, she had sewn on to it a gross of diamantes in order to give it glitter, and the claws of the diamante had caught in the lace, snagging and pulling the dress down, which she blamed on us for not fitting it properly! She was the only customer for whom I opened the door and asked her politely to leave. As she did so, she uttered threats as to what she would do to our reputation. In the event, everyone thought it was a great joke, but I was saddened to see a good piece of work ruined through her stupidity.

One of the saddest episodes concerned a pedantic lady who brought in some suiting for us to make a skirt. It was at the time when fabric manufacturers were starting to experiment with mixing yarns, and as yet no laws had been formulated to make it obligatory to state the content of the fabric, declaring the yarns of which it was made. Clearly in retrospect it must have had a sizeable content of nylon. In the event, the side seams would not lie as flat as in a woollen suiting. She returned with the skirt and complained. Now the side seams were stitched with paper underneath, which was then pulled away, so as to loosen the stitch and avoid any cockling, but she was still not satisfied. Suddenly, our tailoress Miss Faulkner exploded. She said that she no longer wanted to work for women who were so fickle that a blind man would be glad to see any imperfections. She could not be persuaded to reconsider her decision, so it was a great loss and sadness for us all. She then got a job without responsibility, making overalls at the hospital, close by her home, until she retired a few years later. We kept in touch, as we shared the same birthday. Her sister brought her out to see me on 31st March in the year that she died, and we reminisced happily about the good times, which were many.

This was one of the incidents that reinforced the slogan: "There is no substitute for wool!"

6. *That Special Occasion*

Right from the beginning, weddings featured prominently, but an early disaster set the pattern and saved us many a heartache. The inquiry was for six bridesmaids only, as the bride was a nurse in London and would get her wedding dress from Harrods. The bride's mother explained what they wanted - really dainty and pretty dresses. There were four grown-up and two little girl bridesmaids, all of whom were beautiful. As it was an August wedding, I designed tiered dresses of white tulle, the design outlined with plaited straw and ears of corn with headdresses to match. They looked as though they had come from a Covent Garden ballet. Everyone was enchanted until the week before the wedding, when the anguished bride's mother phoned to ask if we could do an alteration on the bride's dress, as it didn't quite fit! I could have wept when they came in to the showroom and the bride put on her wedding gown. It was so sad, as it had clearly been exposed to too much light and was now an indeterminate shade of cream. In no way could she be attended by such shining beauties in pristine white. I did what I could, at that late hour, to improve her dress and make it fit. We then had to dismantle all the trimmings from the bridesmaids' dresses and trim them with a matching cream braid, the only trimming that could be found that was the same colour as the bride's dress. The bride's mother was distraught, and I did not see her again. As a result of the wedding, we gained many new customers from that area, as I am sure that the story got around. We learnt a lesson from the whole episode, and from then onwards only agreed to commissions for the whole wedding. In this way we could ensure that the bride was the central figure of her Special Day.

Weddings and evening gowns were to become the backbone of our business. In the early days weddings were still quite frugal affairs, but as time went on they became more and more extravagant events. I remember a wedding at St Paul's Church, Bedford, where the bride wore her grandmother's Edwardian wedding dress. It was a deep cream satin sculptured dress with leg-of- mutton sleeves which were embroidered with a quilted design that was repeated on the skirt . Of course it had to be re-cut and re-made to fit her. She was also quite upset that it had become such a deep cream. However, to complement it, the bridesmaids' dresses were made of a matching deep cream organdie, flocked with snowy white that trailed a similar flower design. They carried coral roses to

The bride with her bridegroom leaving St Paul's Church, Bedford, wears her grandmother's beautiful quilted and embroidered satin wedding gown, with full leg-of-mutton sleeves, - which had been re-modelled for her in the workroom of D'Arcy & Rosamunde.

match velvet cummerbunds, which picked up the colours on the screen of the church.

The most dramatic event occurred when I was dressing one bride. There was an anguished last-minute call from her father, who had failed to try on his hire suit, and the trousers were at least six inches too big for him! I managed to find a thick needle and double black thread to tack a large pleat at the back and suspend them with braces. Fortunately it did not show under his tail jacket, which fitted him correctly, but I hope that there was not another gentleman in even greater distress with trousers that were too small!

Our most glamorous wedding took place in the Chapel of the House of Commons, with the reception being held in the River Room of the Savoy Hotel. Everything was beautiful, the bride was exquisite and the bride's mother looked most elegant. I helped dress the bride and attended the reception, but sadly the marriage did not last for long. A dissertation needs to be written on the difference between *marriage* and *weddings*, but I doubt whether anyone would bother to read it. The week before the wedding, tensions were often clearly visible in our showroom, and much patience and diplomacy was necessary in order to resolve difficult situations. Early on, both Estelle and I resolved that we would never have a big wedding!

By reputation, glamorous weddings became our core business, with queues of brides' and bridesmaids' dresses hanging in the workroom. Many Saturdays I attended a wedding to help dress the bride and see her into church, making sure that her dress was not creased and her train flowed elegantly. It was very satisfying to see the final result of our work.

One bride had the courage to call off her wedding on the day before the occasion, and her parents were furious at the cost and inconvenience that it caused. Guests had flown in from Hong Kong and around the world to attend the wedding. Telegrams had to be sent all over the country to prevent as many guests as possible from arriving. I felt sorry for her father when he collected and paid for the wedding dress on the day before the wedding was due to take place. It was sad to see him rolling up our beautiful workmanship in a tight ball in his anger. I was glad that the seamstress who made the wedding gown did not witness the scene. It was bad enough for me, but would have been heartbreaking for her, after working on the gown for some weeks and lavishing on it so much of her time, loving care and attention.

During the period in which I was designing wedding gowns, a strapless dress was not considered decorous or acceptable to wear in a church. Therefore, although strapless dresses were made to wear as evening gowns afterwards, a long sleeved bolero or overdress was always made to demurely cover the shoulders and arms in church.

Weddings gowns were not always conventional. One Christmas wedding was very glamorous with the bride in a ballerina length dress, made of a deep turquoise organza with white chenille spots, which looked like falling snow. Instead of the usual bouquet she carried a white fur muff with a spray of flowers attached to it. Finally, to complete the picture, she wore a matching white fur hat to frame the face. It was quite enchanting.

A beautiful bride has her train and veil arranged as she leaves the bridal car and starts on her way up the church path.. Thankfully it was a glorious day - BUT there were always lots of golf umbrellas standing by for those brides who were not so fortunate. A strong wind was the greatest hazard, either knotting up the veil or worse still making it catch in the branch of a tree!

The most exquisite wedding gown we created, was made of handmade Irish lace. The bride's mother, who was of Irish origin, requested that I design and make the dress of lace with shamrocks on it! Every wholesaler and store in London was searched to find a lace with shamrocks, but without success. Finally the problem was solved when the bride's mother said that she had arranged that the nuns of Carrickmacross would make the lace for her. The dress was designed and fitted in a fine toile and then the pattern was posted to Ireland. In an amazingly short time, the lace was returned, appliqued on to nylon tulle in the most amazing design. When I saw the intricate workmanship, I was sad that it had been made on nylon tulle instead of a pure silk organza, as the life of tulle is very short, but it would probably have taken the dress over budget.

The design of the gown had the hem edged with a random design of flowers and knotted shamrocks. Then the pattern trailed up into the skirt. The neckline of the bodice and the point over the hand of the long sleeves were edged with a cathedral scallop. Finally, a full bouffant short veil was edged with a smaller version of the same design. The nuns obviously enjoyed making it, as I received letter from them, saying that they appreciated the care with which the pattern had been produced. They also made a handkerchief for me as a memento of the occasion, embroidering it with the same motifs. I treasure it especially because it is the only record of their amazing work on that wedding gown. Later it was shortened to wear as a ballgown, as we knew that it was too fragile to hand down for future generations.

This handkerchief was made by the nuns of Carrickmacross as a memento for Thelma, using the same motifs as for the wedding gown. The neckline, hems of the sleeves and the veil were edged with shadow embroidered cathedral scallops as seen on the handkerchief.

7. Next to Nellie

Each September we took at least one new apprentice to train in the workroom. Mostly they stayed until they got married, as it was the custom in those days to give up work, make a home and start a family. One or two continued to work for a short while, but I used to get quite despondent when we lost a good hand in this way. From their point of view, with our training, they could work from home and always get more work than they needed or wanted.

A new apprentice was quite a responsibility, and it was vital to get to know her as soon as possible. She was given the job, to fill in odd minutes whilst waiting for instruction, of making shoulder clips with white, pale pink, pale blue and black narrow ribbon. Most dresses had shoulder clips stitched into them, since, even when wearing an afternoon "frock", couture customers liked to have their shoulder straps secured firmly, so that they did not slip down the arm! With evening and cocktail gowns it was vital—it was considered infra dig to show a shoulder or bra strap. As standards have slipped over the years, it is amazing to recall the attention given to every little detail in the 1950s, as can be seen in the photograph of the bride alongside on this page.

Every garment made in our workroom had a D'Arcy label stitched into it with a herringbone stitch, whilst each of the ready-to-wear garments, of which hundreds arrived each season, had a D'Arcy & Rosamunde label stitched into it. This

This is a typical bride of the 1950s. Her gown is close-fitting lace with see-through lace sleeves, which point over the hands. Her neckline is high and demure, but the bodice is also see-through and only lined through the strapless top. She has the traditional tiny buttons up the sleeve and down the front of the bodice. Her many-layered full skirt of net is held out on stiff petticoats and is cut longer at the back so as to drag almost into a train. The full short tulle veil echoes the shape of the dress.

resulted in quite a steady job for the apprentice, although everyone else helped. Each of the seamstresses liked to work on different types of garment, and to achieve the best result it was wise to find out their preferences. It was usually the nature of the fabric that determined their choice. Some would like to work on woollens, could handle heavy irons and liked moulding the fabric, whilst others preferred more delicate work, with an emphasis on hand sewing. Chiffon required particularly gentle handling, because our aim was to create dresses that looked as though they had been blown together rather than firmly stitched, which of course they had to be! Pure silk chiffon dresses did not withstand very well the rigours of wearing, so there were none in our collections, as they were always made to order. With the advent of man-made fabrics, chiffons became more practical but they did not move in the same way as pure silk. All chiffon edges were nevertheless rolled and hemmed by hand. Betty and Eileen were probably our finest seamstresses for handling delicate fabrics. Often customers would arrive back from a visit to India, bringing with them gossamer-fine sari fabrics, wanting them made into European-style dresses. I would explain that the fabric was not designed to be sewn into fitted clothes, but with careful design and mounted on fine but firm cotton, many beautiful dresses were made.

During the middle of the 1950s, a customer told us of a lady who had worked for her for many years but wanted to find a job sewing. I was a little reluctant to take on someone who had not been professionally trained, but the customer was so persistent and full of extravagant praise in her recommendation that I gave way. How pleased we were that I did so! Mrs Dowler joined us, and

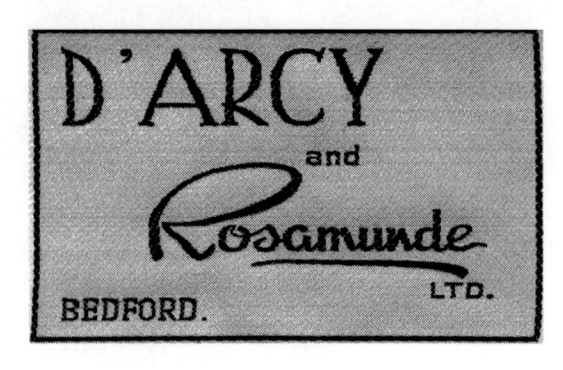

Our distinctive name came about as a result of the joining together of the name D'Arcy, which I had registered as a trade name when starting up in business on my own, being added to Rosamunde, the original name of the business.

Our label was made of heavy silver grey satin with the names embroidered in cyclamen silk.

One of the characters who regularly visited the workroom was the knife sharpener. He came on his bicycle, which had been converted so that he could jack it up and use the pedal motion to turn a stone for sharpening. For only a few pence each, he would sharpen all the scissors for us. It is amazing to think that he made a living in those days, going from house to house sharpening knives and scissors.

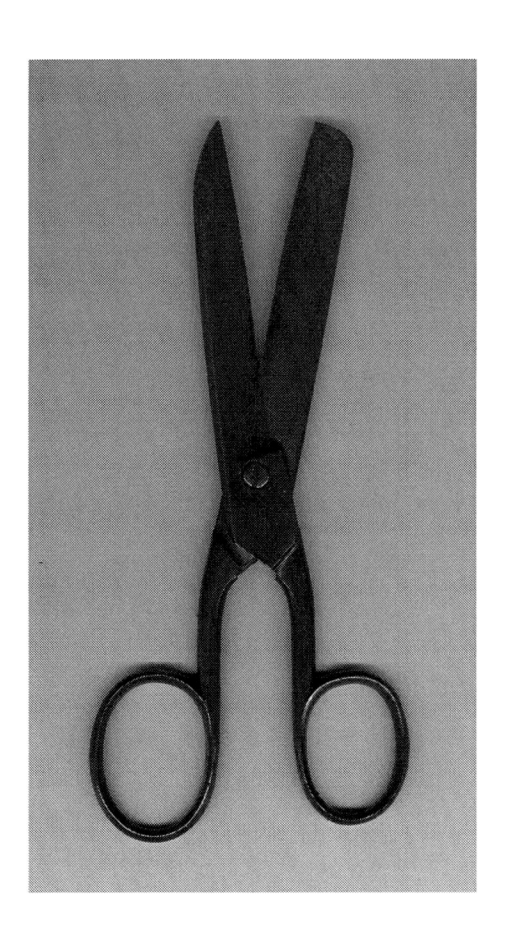

picked up our ways immediately. Not only that, she became a mother figure in the workroom and a liaison person for everyone long before personnel managers became the vogue. She could turn her hand to anything, being immensely practical in every way. Often she had a solution to a problem before anyone else had thought about it. When my sister and I had our children, she delighted in taking them to her home to teach them how to make pastry. She taught each of them how to use a sewing machine and my son Roger could sew as well as any of the girls. She could double up as a salesperson in the showroom and soon learnt the art of simple fitting. Eventually she worked for D'Arcy & Rosamunde for over twenty- five years.

Over the period that we trained apprentices in the workroom, many youngsters were employed. I particularly remember Eileen, who in her quiet way held very strong opinions. She was one of the early girls to prove that I was wrong in my expectation that girls did not continue to work after they were married. Sadly, she suffered with ill health and died at a young age. She was a superb seamstress.

It needed great patience to get through the first six months of an apprenticeship, as the workroom worked on the "Next to Nellie" method. This meant that the apprentice sat alongside an experienced hand and must make a sampler of whatever process was needed, before being let loose on a garment for a customer. Stitching on press-fasteners and hooks and eyes with a blanket stitch in a tidy and secure manner was the first task. Then followed yards of oversewing by hand, each stitch being the same size and depth. The introduction of the zigzag on the sewing machine gave release from this drudgery, as ordinary overlocking was not acceptable in the world of couture, and only used in mass-production. By the end of six months the apprentice should have made a woollen skirt, and by the end of the year a blouse. At the end of two years, the apprenticeship was then complete, but it was considered necessary to have worked for fifteen years to be competent in handling all fabrics as a tailor. So experience was gained over a long period. Gradually each girl developed her skill in handling different fabrics and they all specialised in different directions. I was extremely proud of our team, and most of the girls stayed with us until they married. Later on one of the girls, Joan, developed her own successful business, but each of the girls had a skill which she could use at home to supplement her income. The skills of a couture dressmaker are always in demand, and there were always girls waiting to be trained.

The "Next to Nellie" form of training and apprenticeships were looked down upon by those who went to technical colleges. Only now is it realised that there are many for whom textbook learning is not appropriate, and who find practical demonstration to be of more value. We found that many of those of a practical bent, once motivated, achieved manual skills, then developed a self-esteem which enabled them to progress in other directions. Many of these girls became our most valued seamstresses because, once taught, they would not devise ways to cut corners. In other words, they could always be trusted to maintain our standards. In many cases the story of The Hare and the Tortoise proved true, with the slower girl arriving at the finishing post, without any mistakes, whilst those who rushed through their work had to retrace their steps to achieve the same accuracy.

Detail of a sampler of embroidery stitches done by Thelma during her training.

8. My Formative Years

During the austerity of the Second World War, there was little opportunity for experimentation until I was given an old, used parachute when I was around the age of fourteen. It was huge, and enabled me to indulge my designing fantasies of underwear and a flowing nightdress. Before that, when I was about twelve, navy serge had been supplied to my parents to have made for me a uniform dress for school. I enquired what style it should be and was told, just a fitted bodice and flared skirt. Imagine when I arrived at school, wearing a princess-line dress with a fitted bodice and flared skirt, but buttoned through with enormous white clown-like buttons! I was scolded, but there was nothing that the nuns could do, as cloth was severely rationed during the war, and it was impossible to find any large navy buttons.

When I set off for college in London, I needed a warm winter coat. So my mother had her old turquoise Harris tweed coat "turned" and re-made to fit me by the local tailor. It was quite amazing, as the fabric had worn thin in places on the right side, but once "turned" to the other side it looked like new cloth, bright in colour with a fluffy surface. The only tell-tale signs were some shiny iron marks where it had been originally pressed on the wrong side. So at least I was reasonably warm when I arrived in bombed-out London in 1946, a city without any heating. Each day when I left college at five o'clock, I would go to Selfridges for half an hour to warm up. Although there was no heating in the store, the residue of body heat from the crowds during the day made it feel warmer than the hostel. Many of the stores had not been rebuilt after being bombed, so the only other store close by was Debenham & Freebody in Wigmore Street, but that was an up-market shop and did not attract the crowds. In any case, I felt rather conspicuous and inappropriate there, as I was clearly not a potential customer.

There was great excitement at college when we were told that we were to visit Worth, the fashion house, then situated at Oxford Circus. This would be our first visit to a fashion show, and I had no idea what to expect. The architecture of the Circus is really beautiful and at that time it was an elegant part of London. We arrived at the building on the north-west corner, entered through beautifully polished glass doors, and were taken up a regal curved stone staircase to the showroom on the first floor. There, lined up in rows on the gleaming parquet floor, were little gold- painted chairs. Soon, an elegant compère appeared to tell us about Worth's 1947 Spring collection, before the tall models began to pirouette along a central strip of carpet. There was no music except the noise of the traffic below, but the sun seemed to add to the spotlights which lit up the fashions. The colours were mostly navy with acid lime green, lemon or white. Lilies-of-the- valley were scattered extravagantly, and I was entranced. In the Spring of 1947, Dior had just produced his New Look, so everyone had followed his lead—skirts were almost ankle length with waists that were cinched. It was very glamorous and exciting after the dreariness of the wartime fashions.

Gradually, from then onwards, new fabrics appeared, although they were always in short supply. Ration coupons were needed to buy a length of fabric, so apart from finding the money, a

This was the very first evening gown that I made whilst still at college. Someone discovered that if you were a farmer, you could buy up to five yards of cotton organdie at a time without coupons, from the Co-op for milk-straining. So as I came from a farming family, this was not difficult to arrange. And once I'd purchased ten yards of white cotton organdie, the dress was a very economical proposition!

great deal of thought was needed before splashing out to spend those precious coupons. Always there was the thought, though, that things were getting better all of the time. It was a period of hopeful anticipation. After the show, every student lashed out and made a New Look dress for herself, and we paraded around in them, defiantly wearing purple lipstick!

Our studies at college covered a wide spectrum, from The History of Costume, which I found fascinating, through to the modern technicalities of cutting and manufacture of wholesale clothing. We were the last group to study couture dressmaking and French modelling, as it was an aspect of fashion which was fast disappearing. Thankfully I recall that it was the most important part of my training for my years at D'Arcy & Rosamunde. Then we studied the human body through Life Drawing, which led us on to pattern making and sizing. These were vital skills and included patterns for both historic costumes and children's wear. Designing by learning about the form from Life Drawing from the human figure caused much hilarity because of the motley group of models who appeared. Did anyone really have figures like that? And finally, the writing of business letters and preparing a balance sheet to trial-balance stage completed the course. We were stimulated by outside visiting lecturers, amongst them the new young designer, Hardy Amies. He had just started business on his own but as yet had not gained Royal patronage. I recall that his enthusiasm inspired us all.

Later I enrolled for a course in tailoring in Savile Row. I also continued my art training at St Martin's College of Art, where I attended a Life Drawing class twice a week, as well as studying Advertising

Design and the Art of Lettering. Meanwhile, in order to get experience of working for a theatrical designer, as soon as the course was finished, I took a job with Joy Ricardo in Hans Crescent in Knightsbridge, working in a dark basement room of an elegant house as a seamstress at £3.00 per week. The first dress on which I worked belonged to Deborah Kerr, who had many dresses in the making. I recall that she sent in a huge box of biscuits to the workroom in appreciation of our work, which was gratefully received because food was still rationed. We thought that she must have brought them back from Hollywood. It is a matter of some pride that I was also asked to deliver a dress that I had made for Anne Crawford by taxi to the stage door of a theatre for her first night. So I was even more thrilled to see her photographed wearing it in the Evening Standard, with a comment about the neckline! After six weeks, I received ten shillings (50 pence) increase in my wages, but after three months I decided that I wanted to be designing and there was no hope of doing so in this Knightsbridge establishment.

On my return to college, another job was immediately found for me on the strength of my fashion drawing, this time to design display cards for a well known wholesale firm at a salary of £6.00. The company sent me on a course to learn how to silk-screen print, later putting me in the charge of their advertising agent, with whom I got on very well. I was thrilled to find that I had my own little studio on the top floor of the building. My work for the season was given to me and I was left to my own devices. My designs seemed always to be appreciated and accepted, so I worked away steadily at the job. Washing off the paint on a screen in the middle of a job was so time-consuming, I nearly always worked through

Detail from a silk-screened show card to promote STEPHANY models.

my lunch hour. As a result, my work was finished two weeks before the end of the season. So, on reporting to the director, I was told to visit the art galleries to get ideas for the next season. This really was my dream job, but it was not to last.

My mandate was to produce advertising that gave the impression of the firm's style without featuring any particular garment. After two seasons, the customers commented that they preferred my impressions to the actual collection, so I was invited to design half a dozen outfits for the following Spring season. That was when my troubles began. Leftover fabrics from the previous summer season were given to me and one of my designs proved to be the winner of the season. This caused endless trouble. Far more orders were taken than could be filled with the available fabric, so a substitute had to be found, which was not easy. It also caused jealousy among the other designers. From then onwards, the senior designer made sure that my designs were sabotaged to make sure that it did not happen again.

So after eighteen months (which I was told by my father would be the minimum time that it was decent to be employed this time, otherwise I would get a bad name), it was time to move on. My next application was for the job using silk-screening skills at the fifth largest timber company in the country. The interview was in smart offices in Holborn. No one told me at the time that I would have to work at the end of a muddy lane, out in the back of beyond in a Nissen hut at Hanwell. But the money was good at £7.50 a week. So I took the empty underground train to west of London and found the whole period a great learning curve. The managing director of the Anglo Timber & Trading Company had been in an aircrew in the RAF with an artist during the war. As a result of their discussions, a separate company had been formed to use all the offcuts of the timber to make display stands. I was engaged as personal assistant to the artist, to help with their design and manufacture. Most of the stands were made for the motor and cosmetic industries. I acted as quality controller for all aspects of their production, so learnt about carpentry, sanding and spraying, before I was able to finish them with the silk-screening. There needed to be no rough edges! Apart from an elderly secretary, I was the only female on the site. I learnt a lot about men, not least that they gossiped just as much as women!

Once again after eighteen months, I began to get itchy feet. Whilst I had been working at Hanwell, I was persuaded to continue to make clothes in the evenings. I did it not just for the money but for the pleasure. Before long, one of my customers persuaded me that I was wasting my time and should start to work for myself. It seemed to me that it was the only way that I should be able to do what I wanted. So I went to Bush House and registered the trade name of D'Arcy. Already I had a few customers in London, and I worked from our flat in Cleveland Square—until that fateful visit to Bedford in November 1951.

So ended my five-year sojourn in London. What a fabulous time I had, in spite of having little money to spend. The experiences gained and the risks taken were the best education for which I could have wished, as well as being very enjoyable. What more could I have asked ?

I recall taking a Number 15 bus one evening and walking to a point east of Tower Bridge on the riverside. There I set up my easel to paint.

The original sketch, showing one of the bollards. The scene is very different today. No cranes or berths now, and the good visibility along the river makes it the ideal site for Thames River Police.

Suddenly a hand took hold of my shoulder firmly. Looking up with surprise, I saw a policeman. "What on earth do you think you are doing?" he said. He then gave me a lecture on the dangers of the area and frog-marched me back to the Number 15 bus whilst telling me never to take such risks again.

Almost every week, we would queue for seats in the "gods" at Covent Garden to see opera or the ballet. It was the time when wonderful new musicals were coming from America—"Oklahoma" and "South Pacific", plus the very English "The Boyfriend". Seats only cost about two shillings. So if we could not get into one production, there was always something else around the corner, and it was all on our doorstep. Living in the West End, we were able to walk everywhere, and as a result got to know London very well. It was a very exciting place to be.

By contrast, travel abroad in 1946 was difficult because of the aftermath of the war. A friend and I did manage to stay for two weeks in Paris at the Collège Franco-Brittanique in Paris University at one time, but ran out of money. Everything had to be achieved on very tight margins, with just one very carefully chosen meal a day and an occasional cup of coffee.

So returning to Bedford, I missed the lights and the life. I managed to stay in London one evening a week after completing my buying, so that I could continue to attend the life class at St Martin's College of Art. To this day I mostly feel invigorated after a visit to London. Just occasionally, I remember and mourn the loss of beautiful clothes and a more elegant and leisurely way of life than can be enjoyed today.

9. The Business Grows

When we started in business, Estelle was eighteen and I was twenty-one. So Estelle signed any doubtful documents in the knowledge that, at that time, she could not be held responsible! She is taller than I am and wore her hair in a bun; and as a result looked the older sister, so it seemed natural. At the time, we worked out that if the business was to pay its way, we must take £1,000 per month. It seemed an impossible figure, and in the first year we only managed a turnover of £5,000! Our salary bill without the two apprentices was just over £20 per week, but our expenses were minimal as we lived at home free of charge. The three of us, my mother, my sister and I travelled together each day from St Neots in my mother's little Standard Nine car. Before long, it was apparent that I needed to work longer hours to get through the work, so we put a divan in the little office, so that I could work late into the night. Sometimes my father would call in at ten or eleven o'clock at night to check that I was all right. Imagine his indignation when he received a solicitor's letter, requesting information about the men who were calling on his daughter at late hours! He immediately sent a suitable reply, as he knew that I was much too engrossed with the work in hand to be involved with boyfriends during the week.

It soon became apparent that it would be necessary to find somewhere suitable for future shows. It was decided to go to the Crofton Rooms in St Cuthbert's Street, where Miss Harding held her very popular dancing classes. Once again offering the hand of co-operation, Dorothy Butler, our

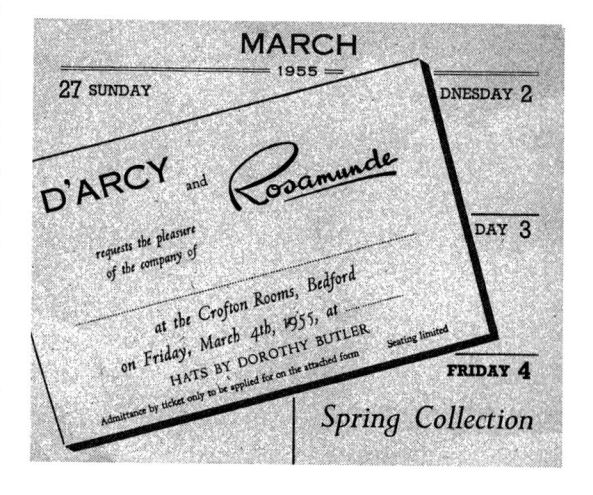

Our invitation was printed on colour like a diary. What an extravagance!

neighbour at the hat shop next door, was invited to join us. Alas, once again, none of her hats seemed to go with our clothes, so the little black dress appeared, for showing all the hats during an interval in the middle of the show. Betty Brierley, who had been a hat model in London, came and went until she was almost dizzy, because showing hats entailed moving the head around like the Gainsborough lady! Bill Kreis, from the music shop Frasers, this time played tunes for us from the shows on a grand piano, so quite a genteel atmosphere was created.

As we became a little more established, we moved from the Crofton Rooms to the Civic Theatre, and on one occasion to the Corn Exchange. Shows were also taken out to places like the Ladies Club at the American airbases at Alconbury and Molesworth, but it involved a great deal of work. Eventually we managed to finance an extension to the showroom to join it on to the workroom, which made life a lot easier. Thus we were able once more to keep the shows "in house", which was a much more practical solution.

Now set up at No 42 Harpur Street, Bedford, with a ready-made workroom but no money, our task was to build a reputation as quickly as possible. I was in my element, so it was no hardship to work both night and day. I continued to have a good social life at the weekends, but refused to get seriously involved with anyone. My parents had an unhappy relationship, and I felt that there was safety in numbers. There was one companion of whom I was very fond and who gave me a lot of support, but I knew in my heart that there was no possibility of a long-term relationship. Generally I was happy as a career girl, designing and making elegant clothes. Quality and good design were the basis of our business. We used the best fabrics that could be found. It was a heady period, as new and exciting fabrics came onto the market. Mikki Sekers was the most inventive fabric manufacturer, producing both silks for cocktail and evening dresses and the most beautiful mohairs, threaded with jewel-coloured narrow velvet ribbons, which we made into glamorous duster coats. Miss Faulkner and I worked together to produce both coats and suits from the wonderful new fabrics that were becoming available. She contributed her immense experience to my imagination. We were a great team, and I would constantly wonder at how frugally she would cut out the linings, never to waste an inch of fabric. In turn I only bought the minimum of fabric for the garment and left her to ingeniously piece together the facings. The war had deprived us of these luxuries for so long that thrift was still the order of the day. Even the men were affected, as husbands persuaded us to make waistcoats for them in jewel-coloured moleskin. So we became an early unisex business.

Glamorous full-length evening gowns were worn to all the local balls, but by the end of this decade the shorter ballerina-length dress became more fashionable. The same length was worn for cocktail dresses, in spite of the casualwear creeping in. I remember how daring I felt when I attended a cocktail party in a tight pair of black trousers for the first time. This was freedom, and it gave me a taste of the attitudes which were to be ushered in with the 1960s.

In the 1950s stockings were still normally worn and had seams down the back, and it was always necessary to make sure that the seams were straight. Later the choice came to have seamless stockings or tights, but it was thought that seams

This was how my feather hat looked!

Hats in the 1950s were fun

and there were still milliners in most towns who could make a bespoke hat for you. A basic matched hood of fine straw or felt could be ordered. A hood looked like a large pudding basin shape! This was then steamed and pulled over one of a number of shaped blocks to make the hat of your choice. Or the milliner might use plaited straw. There was also an enormous variety of trimmings from which to choose.

made the legs look slimmer, so the seamed variety continued to be made for some considerable time. A great deal of attention was given to the way in which a well-dressed person was turned out. Gloves and hats were worn by many, even to go shopping, and certainly it was necessary if you were visiting London for the day. It was said that you could tell the age of a person by her hairstyle and hats, as most women continued to wear the styles of their teens and twenties into their later years. So by the time that I appeared on the fashion scene just after the war, there were many women still wearing the cloche and turban hats of the 1920s and 1930s. These hats were not very flattering, to say the least, and were best typified by Nora Batty in the television series "Last of the Summer Wine". As a reaction, the hats of the 1950s were really coquettish! Many were confections of nonsense, made of flowers, net and feathers. I recall that one of my hats was trimmed with two pheasant tail feathers set horizontally, which tickled the face of bystanders if they came too close to me. It caused much hilarity most of the time, although I was occasionally asked to remove it. Shoes were glamorous. The comfortable variety were only worn in the country or by old ladies. Hairstyles were neat and formal, most people still having a regular perm. It was not until the end of the decade that back-combing gradually appeared as a fashion. It had always been used, but only by those with very thin hair.

Transport in the 1950s gradually improved. I did not get my own transport until 1956, when a customer, who was the wife of a solicitor, told me of an old lady who had died and left a car which had never been out in the dark. It had only made the journey to the cemetery to visit her husband's grave, so was a good purchase for someone. I

The green and black 1936 Morris 8 which we christened the " Dinghy ". It served me well for ten years and was then sold for the same price as it was purchased ! Inflation had arrived.

acted immediately, and was able to buy the 1936 Morris Eight for the sum of £50. It proved a trusty vehicle. At about the same time, another customer, who was the wife of the main motor agent in the town, had a dark green suit made to match their new streamlined car that had just arrived, to wear as she took part in a concourse d'elegance. Today, we take for granted the comfort and general standard of reliability of cars, but it was not so in those days.

The autumn of 1958 was very special for me. I was invited to join a group of buyers, sponsored by Vogue magazine, on a trip to Paris to visit the couture houses for their shows. It was both a great opportunity and a great honour, as there were only two independent buyers in the party—a lady from York and myself. Most of the party were buyers from the well known London stores. I think that it may have been because I had the reputation for refusing to buy the mainstream winners of the collections from the wholesale collections which went into every store. Rather, I would find something special that perhaps others had missed and later everyone wondered why.

We stayed at the Hotel Cité Bergère, and it was the first time that I had been greeted with a bouquet of red roses in my bedroom! Then followed four hectic days, when we were taken around the city by taxi. We visited Chanel, a shimmering showroom, consisting of all mirrors and chrome; Christian Dior, which was closely guarded but had tremendous flair, and the display was fantastic whilst Carven did not appeal to me, as it seemed very contrived and the clothes appeared to be badly made! It is the fashion house that is famous for the perfume called Ma Griffe. At Pierre Balmain I was to meet Madame Ginette Spanier for the

The rotund figure of Chef Georges prepares our starter at the table.

first time. She had that gift for making everyone that she met feel special. The collection, which had the reputation for being wearable, was not memorable, but very elegant for the conventional lady. I think that Balmain had the largest private clientèle in Paris at the time. Jacques Heim in the Avenue Matignon was the collection which appealed to me most of all. It was presented with loving care, and his hats and furs were exquisite. Here I was presented with a handbag phial of his perfume called J'Aime, which soon became my favourite. Roger & Gallet's showroom in the Faubourg St Honoré was made of mirrors and chicken wire. Here I was given a glass candlestick filled with a spicy cologne. The Directrice told us: "Never worry about being copied. Imitation is the most sincere form of flattery."

Chef Georges, who was one of the original "celebrity chefs", with his guests towards the end of the evening. There had been much banter, singing and fun.
To the right is the "King of the Evening", an antique dealer from Majorca, next to Thelma as the "Queen" and an American as the Pope.

In the evenings, we dined out. We visited the Folies Bergère and had a memorable evening at the Rotisserie de la Table du Roi of a notable television personality, Le Chef Georges. As the parties arrived at appropriate intervals, they were met by Le Chef Georges, who would chat with the members and then design and prepare a special starter for them. The main course was standard, usually consisting of pheasant or partridge, served with panache on swords, by pageboys. Finally, when the place was full, Chef Georges conducted a concert party involving the guests. Here I was crowned Queen of the Evening and drank too much champagne! The King was an antique dealer from Majorca, and the Pope was an amusing American. It was great fun; the Chef Georges was quite a personality!

By 1960 I wondered where fashion could go to improve on what had been a very elegant decade. The wait was not long. Biba and Mary Quant burst on the British fashion scene with mini-skirts. There had been the introduction of the sack dress in 1957 by Balenciaga, which brought in a more relaxed shape. This design was then taken up by other designers, notably Givenchy and Jacques Griffe, and it was the dominant line by 1960. I can recall that we made a dress of actual sackcloth for Estelle to wear at one of our shows. Another D'Arcy sackcloth dress that proved very popular was buttoned through the front with miniature clothes-pegs. However, the lady who bought it was very irate because she later saw that there was another one in the window. We had to explain to her that she could not expect exclusivity on a dress that was costing less than £10. So there had been indications that change was on the way.

We aimed for an ageless elegance, and Estelle was always our star model at the shows. Apart from her looks and figure, this was on account of her sharp hearing and quick wit. Customers would whisper a comment, which nine out of ten times Estelle would hear and respond to, with a wicked sense of humour. She would model the size 14, although we abandoned sizing for psychological reasons, following the example of the French

A compromise from MUNROSPUN for the countrygirl.

house Tricosa. If you were a size 14, you were a "two star", but if you were a size 20, then you were a "five star" and felt very grand as a result. Our three-star model (size 16) was always very popular, and we usually had a short fitting model (size 12) as well, often my deputy Monica Wilkinson. One of our most charming grey-haired models was Mrs East, who ran a skating school in London. She was a true example of how attractive and agile the older woman could be. She, in fact, showed the outfit that Elizabeth Arden bought to wear at Ascot.

As we approached the end of the 1950s, I looked back on a golden Age of Elegance. It was glamorous, it was elegant, and fashion was affordable. It was a great pleasure to shop for clothes, because there was an enormous variety from which to choose. There were lots of beautiful art shades of colour, even tweeds were dyed into soft turquoise, amethyst, jade, maize and soft rose pink. Claire Cobden produced a long woollen tweed duster coat with a matching lighter-weight sheath dress for around 29 guineas, (£29 and 29 shillings, i.e. £30 9s). We sold many of these outfits, which were wearable for many occasions.

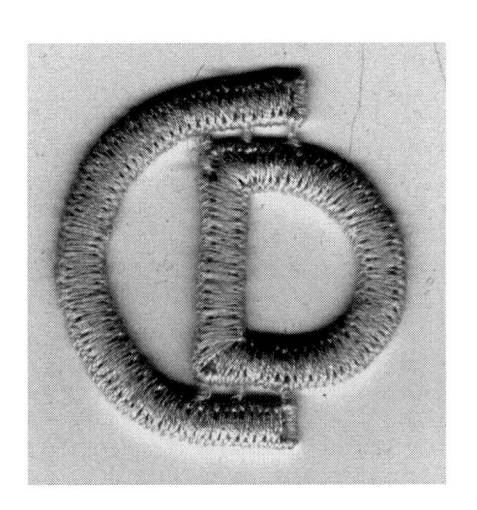

Norman Hartnell teamed up with Christian Dior to market their own ready-to-wear collections. I enjoyed visiting Hartnell's sumptuous showroom in Bruton Street in London's West End to make our selections, for we stocked them both. Suddenly logos were being worn on the outside of garments —a phenomenon that had never before been seen! Many folk never expected to afford a Dior outfit, so the logo was cut off and treasured before a garment was passed on to a second-hand shop. Sadly the ready-to-wear collections were only produced for a few seasons, as it was difficult to keep both ends of a business going together, because they don't

The Christian Dior logo

mix very well. Although the two were different, I should not be very happy if I were buying the expensive bespoke version from the salon in Paris or London, only to see the same name blazoned in all of the stores.

At this time, great strides were made in refining and broadening the scope of knitwear. Much of the Dior's ready-to-wear collection was made of knitted fabrics. Many outfits had fine all-round pleated skirts with soft jumper tops. Another firm, Playfair, imported from Italy a wide range of jackets and jumpers, ranging from tailored heavy-knit jackets to gossamer-fine evening tops with Lurex. Suddenly it was found that these garments did not crease and were easy to wear for travelling. The practicality of this new knitwear, with the upmarket look, made it an instantaneous winner.

Also from Italy, printed pure silk jersey opened our eyes to the most wonderful colour combinations, which could only be mixed in the bright sunlight of the southern sun. Added to that, the fabric was so fine that it was alleged that a dress could be pulled through a wedding ring. I did not try, and remain a little incredulous!

Fabulous fashion jewellery became available, mostly imported from Austria. We stocked a large selection, and depended on it to enhance cocktail and evening wear. We also sold an enormous amount at Christmas for presents, for some pieces were really beautiful and stood in their own right as fashion jewellery.

Looking back over the 1950s, I realise that the ritual of buying a new suit and hat to wear at church on Easter Day still allowed us to buy with confidence. A Spring coat was also still a necessary purchase, usually bought in a practical shade of cream or camel so that it could be worn over anything.

In Spring 1953 the glossy fashion magazine L'Officiel showed the daring swimming costumes and corsetry of the day. I can recall that at college, we students all made ourselves cotton two-piece swimsuits with a *bare* midriff—the forerunner of the bikini,—and felt very daring because a one-piece swimsuit with an overskirt was thought to be more decorous and modest to wear!

In the evening, a cinched waist still did not cause too much problem, as food was rationed until 1954. Thus when you went out for an evening there was not much to eat. I remember clearly when it became possible to cater properly at dances, rather than being offered just a fish-paste sandwich. There was great excitement when meringues and eclairs were first seen. Generally speaking, people drank more heavily during the war, and there were no drink-drive laws in those days. Dodging an inebriated partner was an important art to acquire. Before the advent of gin and tonic, gin and orange, sherry or Dubonnet were the usual drinks for a girl. Most of the men drank beer or whisky, or the Americans—many of whom remained—would drink whisky followed by beer as a "chaser", which was a lethal mix.

Most of the 1950s was a period of hope. Everything was getting better all the time for most people. There were still boarded-up bomb sites to remind you of the dark days of the Second World War, and the deprivations were still clear in the memory.

A lace wedding gown at the final fitting, with Ann Bambridge and Estelle Addington holding the train.

10. The End of an Era

In January 1959 I met David Marks, and we were married in September. Thus a new era began. Estelle had married three years earlier and already worked part-time. Now it was time to look at my working practices (and learn to cook!).

A visit to my old college in London proved very fruitful, as Monica Wilkinson [who lived in Luton] had just finished her college course. She joined us immediately as cutter and fitter, and I gradually withdrew from the day-to-day running of the workroom. In the beginning, Miss Faulkner found it difficult to accept someone new in that capacity but Miss Wilkinson, as she was then known, was such a lovely character that the problem was soon overcome.

Mrs Philcox, a very talented Italian lady, joined us as a sales assistant and took over the display in the showroom. We worked well together, and this relieved me of another aspect of my work. She was a great asset to the business in many ways, as she was full of ideas and could turn her hand in many directions. She was warm and vivacious; there was usually lots of laughter in the showroom when she was around. Later, when she had problems and her family was in Italy, my mother became an adoptive mother to her.

Mrs Allen, Miss Craig and other valued staff joined us in the showroom over the years, whilst in the office, Estelle had a variety of help at different times to look after the books and money. As the numbers grew, the cellars were decorated and heated to make a canteen where everyone could have their coffee. Soon a cooker was installed, and

Monica Wilkinson at the cutting table with her scissors.

someone employed to prepare a simple lunch. Always during the shows, everyone was fed on the premises, even from the early days. My mother would cook a huge turkey, which was served hot on the first evening, then available sliced cold with salads, and finally the last bits—made into vol-au-vents for the final evening. There were sweets and cheese and biscuits as well, so no one went hungry! It became a much appreciated tradition.

In the 1960s I think that it is true to say that, with my husband David's help, we became more proficient. Our initial training in London had ensured that we were professional in running the business, employing London models for the shows and buying from the best houses, but we now began to analyse our regular working practices. Whilst the workroom was our best advertisement, it was not highly profitable. As the wages went up, it became apparent that unless we were able to be more efficient, that aspect of the business would be at risk. The zigzag sewing machine had eliminated the need to oversew by hand, but we did not drop our standards otherwise. In the slack time we made a limited number of garments for stock.

Alterations were also a liability, as our standards were very high. I can recall one very large young customer who desperately wanted a dress for a special occasion. Of course, her size was not immediately available from any manufacturer, and there was not really time for us to make anything for her. So in desperation we ordered two very pretty large-size dresses, cut them through and joined them together very successfully. We went to great lengths—and widths—to satisfy our customers!

David and Estelle

Following the family tradition of a quiet wedding, Estelle married David Addington early one morning at Roxton Church in 1956 and Thelma followed suit by marrying David Marks at Eaton Socon Church in 1959.

About this time we also took over the lease of the hat shop next door at No. 40. This enabled us to increase our accessories and synchronise the stock, although we had not considered the problems of staffing a separate shop, as there were no connecting doors.

> In 1964 my father died, leaving the farm to my mother, who ran it for a short while before running into some problems. So she handed it over to my sister and me, who then had the challenge of learning how to run a farm! A relative reassured us that if you can run one business, with appropriate professional help you can run any business.
>
> Estelle once again handled the finances, and I went to Caxton every Thursday to pay the wages and keep up to date with the progress. It could be a little confusing. I am rather absent-minded, and have been known to ask for an acre of cloth. We were also teased that we were the only farmers with lace curtains in the tractor windows!
>
> Eventually we realised that the income from a small farm could not justify buying the necessary machinery to run it, so we teamed up with a cousin, who agreed to run the farm, and a contracting company, so that the machinery could earn its way on other farmers' farms.
>
> This was a happy arrangement, and we kept the farm for fifteen years, until we felt the wind of change coming in agriculture. The farm was sold in 1983, one year following D'Arcy & Rosamunde, and we were free of responsibilities for the first time since 1951.

We would bend over backwards in trying to accommodate our customers, and most of them appreciated our service. In fact as I meet them in the town, there is the continual comment: "How we miss you," which is nice to know.
Yes, I too miss the human companionship of the business world, as painting is a solitary occupation, but I am never lonely. I feel privileged to have lived in that period of history when most people were happy.

11. The Swinging Sixties

The Swinging Sixties focused entirely on youth, and fashion for that age group became affordable. The length of skirts rose above the knee in 1961, and by 1966 had reached the upper thigh. The mini-skirt was an instant success. It took little fabric to make, and therefore cost little to buy. London suddenly became a centre for fashion, with Mary Quant, who opened Bazaar in the Kings Road, Chelsea, followed by Barbara Hulanicki, who launched the boutique Biba in Kensington High Street, leading the way.

The mini-skirt was originally inspired by the fact that if a skirt was less than a certain length (I cannot remember the exact figure) it was classed as children's wear and did not attract purchase tax. Thus began a new "way-out" mode of dressing for the young and not so young. I can recall walking down Bond Street at the time when everyone was turning their heads to look at these very short skirts. In front of me was a very kinky "girl", but when she turned round it proved to be Polly Peck, a very well known dress designer of indeterminate age. It looked rather sad, but it has to be said that this new way of dressing heralded the end of the "middle-aged woman", previously thought of as being in her forties to sixties. We had entered the Swinging Sixties, when anyone of any age could wear anything -- at least in theory.

Suddenly a visit to Carnaby Street, at the back of Liberty's, was necessary in order to see this London fashion revolution. It had become the centre for men's fashion, which had become more flamboyant and colourful than within living memory. Earlier generations had been quite conservative, but the young now threw all their inhibitions to the wind and once again in history men were peacocks. The French fashion houses and much of continental Europe largely ignored this London trend, as did D'Arcy & Rosamunde. We conceded by showing representative items in our fashion shows, but seldom were they sold. It was necessary to maintain our quality, so we only included model garments, and then the price was too high for the young. In any case, many of our customers thought it was in bad taste to dress in this way.

In 1960, Princess Margaret married a commoner, Anthony Armstrong-Jones. Her fairytale dress adhered to the standards of the 1950s. In the same year the Queen Mother celebrated her 60th birthday. This was the moment when both the Queen and the Queen Mother ossified their wardrobes. From then onwards the Queen was only able to follow fashion with her hats, which she wore with great courage as a crown. To this day, she continues to wear fashions prevalent at the end of the 1950s. It would probably be true to say that many of our customers followed suit.

We made many clothes for people with figure problems. Early breast-cancer patients would suffer with enormous upper arms, caused by having their glands removed. Other people were deformed or had weight problems. These customers presented a challenge. It gave enormous pleasure and satisfaction to conceal their problems and make them feel good about themselves in classic clothes that were a good investment and did not date. With this level of service, our customers were almost guaranteed to return year after year.

Cavalcade of fashion helps campaign

This Victorian walking-out dress with a matching cape was modelled by one of the students from the Bedford Physical Training College.

A couple in Victorian bathing costumes caused laughter at the event which was opened by Mrs Christopher Soames, wife of the MP for Bedford and daughter of Sir Winston Churchill. Other highlights of the show were replicas of the wedding gowns of Princess Alexandra of Denmark, when she married Edward VII, and of Princess Alexandra, who had married Angus Ogilvy earlier in that year.
(See the following page)

In 1963, the girls of the Physical Training College in Bedford asked if we would present a fashion show for them in order to raise funds for the Freedom from Hunger Campaign. They offered to act as models, which seemed a possible idea, so obviously our selection of fashion and reputation appealed to all ages, in spite of the fact that we did not espouse the *way-out* London scene. However, traditionally in all our shows we had always had a comic or amusing interlude of fashion to add a little humour (see the picture alongside). So we arranged to see a group of girls one evening to try on some clothes. Although they were very attractive, imagine our dilemma when none of them was stock size and all of them were young Amazons with magnificently developed muscles! The measurements of the most likely girls were taken and I went away to think. In the end, a fashion show to depict the history of costume was devised, which showed by contrast how modern design repeats old ideas. Thus, professional models were engaged for showing our clothes, whilst costumes to measure from Fox's, the theatrical costumiers, were hired to fit the girls from the Physical Training College. It was a great success, and raised £885 for the charity.

It did not take long for the Paris houses to realise that this London phenomenon was a genuine new trend. André Courrèges produced his Space Age Collection in 1965, which was copied by the wholesale trade for the next season. Samples of his patent look with the white boots were borrowed from the manufacturer and included in our show. Needless to say, no one espoused the look in Bedford! For that matter I cannot recall seeing it being worn in London either. A more successful design was produced by Yves St Laurent in 1965 which was inspired by the modern artist Mondrian. It was a fine white wool worsted shift dress chequered in black with blocks of red and yellow. One or two of this design were sold for cocktail wear. What did become a favourite for all ages from this period was the knee-high white and black boots.

It was quite apparent that great changes were taking place. Suddenly during the 1960s we were shown, and were able to import, beautifully tailored suits from Germany. In 1967 when one of our new manufacturers heard that I was visiting relations in Düsseldorf, he proudly invited me to visit their new factory. The firm was called Nur Kostum, which means Suits Only. How amazed I was to see their new modern factory with no windows. It was pressurised as though you were 10,000 feet up in the mountain scenery, as painted on the walls. There was a canteen and a crèche, both very early innovations at that time. The employees worked very long hours during the height of the season, but between seasons they were able to take much longer holidays than was the norm. They worked in lines, and each suit was broken down into 59 operations, with the detail specified even to the number of stitches on each part of the collar. The design of their suits was classic, with little variation except for fabric colour and detail. This allowed every operation to be mechanised, right down to the pressing. I wondered how we in this country could compete, except perhaps in the men's clothing field, which was able to be treated in a similar way.

However, the company had a business plan that required it to achieve rigid targets in order to pay for its modern installation. Later on its British representative told me that the early seasons went according to plan, but the doubling of orders

The copy of Princess Alexandra's wedding gown shown at the fashion show at the Corn Exchange in aid of the Freedom from Hunger Campaign.

each season became progressively more difficult. Then, quite suddenly, one season our order and his contract were cancelled without notice, and no more was heard of the firm!

Other German firms were much more successful, particularly Ralph of Munich, which was a great favourite of ours, although sadly they too eventually went out of business. Hucke was very reliable and is still there today, whilst Mondi was very popular with the younger customers.

Bedford's past depicted in Charter window display

Mrs Samuel Whitbread, (second from the left), accompanied by the Mayor of Bedford (left) and the president of the Luton Chamber of Trade and his wife, judge the Charter Window displays in Bedford. D'Arcy and Rosamunde were awarded the first prize. In this window can be seen articles which might have been found in an attic, complete with cobwebs and including beams from an 800-year-old church, representing Bedford's past. In the other window were modern articles depicting the Bedford of that day in 1966.

12. Fashion Shows

During the 1950s, fashion shows were our only form of sales promotion. We relied heavily on recommendations, as there was no spare cash for advertising in any other way. However, Spring 1962 was the only season in thirty-one years when we did not have our usual two days of shows. Normally in mid-March each year our Spring Collection was assembled with five consecutive shows over a two-day period, and in early October the same format applied for our Autumn Collection. The three professional models would arrive from London on Monday afternoon for fittings. We just held our breath until we saw them and made sure that they had not changed a size or the colour of their hair! Once they were fitted and the garments put in order, the names for each outfit would be decided, ready for the programme to be printed on the following morning. On many occasions this caused the midnight oil to be burnt! During the Tuesday morning, hurried temporary alterations were made to make sure that the clothes and accessories were appropriate. The first show was at 2.30pm, and another followed at 7.30pm. On the next day there were three shows at 10.30am, 2.30pm and 7.30pm, so it was a hectic week. Customers were able to buy from the shows, so that after each show garments that had been sold were replaced, so each event was a little different. A large part of our turnover was taken during that week. There was no charge for the shows, but a collection was made in aid of Cancer Research after each show. As a result we were able to send regular donations

---

D'Arcy & Rosamunde

At Home

showing their Spring Collection

Tuesday 3rd March
at 2.30pm and 7.30pm

Wednesday 4th March
at 10.30am, 2.30pm and 7.30pm

R.S.V.P   Seating Limited

APPLICATION FOR TICKET
Please fill in Name and Initials as seating is limited and tickets are not transferable

Name--

Address---

Day----------------------------------Time------------------

Day----------------------------------Time------------------

Tickets to our shows were much in demand. We tried to reserve seats for our genuine customers and exclude those who came to just get ideas for home dressmaking, which was still a popular pastime.

A beautifully cut classic dress in wool worsted is worn by Monica.

However, in the third week of March 1962 I was expecting a baby so it was time to produce our first newsletter and Estelle would compère the show instead of modelling. In fact, I was fitting the matron of Bedford Hospital twenty-four hours before Jo arrived and actually booked a fitting for two weeks later, in the knowledge that I had already commenced in labour. I had not expected the baby so soon, but Jo decided to arrive a week early. I could only take two weeks off, as we were already well into the buying season for the following winter!

Estelle had had a daughter, Louise, eighteen months earlier, so we then conveniently took it in turns to be pregnant for the next three years! Louise had a sister, Claire, in 1963 and I had a son, Roger, in 1964. On each occasion whilst pregnant, I stayed in London for a couple of days each week during the buying season, at Brown's in Dover Street or the Durrants in George Street (£4.50 per night). This conserved my energy as the Bedford/London train journey took nearly two hours each way, and travel was not as comfortable as it is today. By 1961 the train fare for a day return ticket had increased to 12 shillings and by 1962 the fare had gone up to 13 shillings (65 pence). Inflation had begun!

After our initial trauma of clearing the previous owner's old stock, it did not take us long to realise that it was imperative not to allow the situation to recur. So at the end of each season there was a short sharp sale when the stock which had not sold was reduced. Initially it was reduced at the end of the first season by one-third; then the following season, it went to half price, and finally, by the third season we almost gave it away in the opening days of a sale.

Our bargains were advertised, and usually there was a queue on the first morning of the sale. There were also customers who liked to buy from us but freely acknowledged that their income did not allow them to pay model prices. They were regular sale customers, many of them teachers. Some would come to the show and ask us to telephone them if their size in a particular model remained by the time of the sale. We were happy to do so, as it helped to keep our stock up to date.

It was also quite galling for us sometimes to see someone come in and find a gem at perhaps a knock-down price, and look magnificent in it. It happened on one occasion when a lady with a model figure like a beanpole arrived and walked into a Dior two-piece. In all the time that it had been in stock, the right person had not appeared in the showroom to try it on. However, we looked on it philosophically, as each outfit had a chance to sell and soon the new stock would be arriving. There must be space for it...

In many ways attitudes changed very quickly in the 1960s. Most people took their skirt length up to the knee and wore simple shift dresses. The nylon revolution had brought easy-care clothes, particularly in stockings and underwear, but the disadvantages were soon apparent. Men's nylon shirts were very unpleasant to wear or sit close by, due to the odour from perspiration. D'Arcy & Rosamunde completely avoided Crimplene and the new synthetic fabrics, but welcomed the mixtures of yarns pioneered by firms like Tricosa, which allowed the fabric to breathe and gave the best of both worlds. Otherwise we continued to specialise in natural fibres, such as cotton, silk and wool.

EXAMPLES OF BARGAINS

Honey gold wild silk Dress & Coat
29gns reduced to 14gns
Beige Suit with printed silk blouse
25gns reduced to 10gns
Jade & pink Tweed Suit with silk facings & blouse,
24gns reduced to 10gns
Embroidered Linen Dress
9gns reduced to 59/6
Printed Pure Silk Dres
10gns reduced to 49/11
Cream silk and wool Dress
16gns reduced to 10 gns
Blue wild silk Dress
19gns reduced to 7 gns
Cotton Dresses
7gns reduced to 89/11
Some discontinued items of knitwear
at greatly reduced prices
Costume jewellery half price.
15% reduction off all models
commencing Wednesday 28th June - 9.30am
TEN DAYS ONLY

D'ARCY & ROSAMUNDE LTD
42 Harpur Street, Bedford Telephone 52157

The prices illustrate the quality and variety of clothes that were available at a modest price in sales of the 1960s. As many people were given money as a present for Christmas, it was vital to get the Christmas display removed and the sale window prepared on Boxing Day, so as to be ready to start the sale on the following morning. Shops closed on Boxing Day but people were window shopping and queued when we opened on the following morning.

SPRING 1969

at

D'ARCY & ROSAMUNDE

The most important development for Spring 1969 was the more fluid line. Skirts were flared, the waistline then being gently indicated with a concave silhouette and maybe a belt.
Colours, according to Vogue: sea blue and sea green (both very flattering colours, especially with a sun tan).
Double-knit textured jersey dress & coat.
Price: - coat 35 guineas - dress: 24 guineas

Shoplifting was a hazard that became more brazen in the 1960s. In the early days when we were unused to the shoplifter's tricks, a group came in the shop and caught our attention, whilst another group followed and managed to clear a whole cupboard of pure silk dresses, complete with coathangers. Only then did we learn that it is impossible to insure against shoplifting. So from then onwards we were much more alert to the possibilities.

Sometimes the police would phone to warn us that a group were on their way from Luton. Then we would close ranks as they entered and say that we had nothing suitable for them. They were usually recognisable by the large shopping bags which they carried.

On another occasion, a man and two women enquired about a coat with a large fur collar. One of the women tried it on and there was much discussion as to whether she would buy it. Then they left. Suddenly we were aware that the coat had disappeared from in front of our eyes! We think that the man must have smuggled it out under his bulky top coat.

One day, an elderly lady stole one earring from the display. Fortunately it was quite inexpensive. Thereafter she kept coming in the shop requesting to look at earrings. We showed the earrings and then the odd earring which we said that she could not have, as someone had stolen the other one. She took the hint, realising that we knew what had happened. She did not come again.

Yet another customer would pay in cash and count out the notes with a great flourish, saying that she was in a hurry. She was very clever, and

*Illustration of the D'Arcy & Rosamunde Showroom - 42 Harpur Street Bedford,
drawn by an advertising agent for the cover of one of our show programme.s*

Dear Readers

Bringing fashion news to you weekly, we have been helped enormously in our presentation by Bedfordshire Times representative Derek Boreham. For fun we have delegated the choice to him this week.

A romantic at heart, he fell for a full-length evening dress in soft caramel, orange and cream tones. Full, gathered sleeves cascade from a slim bodice piped with narrow black braiding. Price £13.50.

caught us out once, but when she tried it again, we insisted on counting out the cash in front of her so as to collect the right amount.

Imports generally increased dramatically in the 1960s, and Tricosa of Paris became our main supplier, accounting for a third of our sales. Their collection was made entirely of jersey fabric, which up until that time had a frumpy image. However, much research and development went into the manufacture of these fabrics, which were made exclusively for them. Tricosa was in the forefront of technology, using the benefits of supple stretch to make for good fitting and comfort. Earlier I had been told in Paris that it is the greatest compliment to be copied *but* it was extremely annoying to see a certain well-known store in every town centre showing a slightly diluted version of a Tricosa model in the following season. In the fashion industry, where design is a development from one season to the next, it is very difficult to prevent this from happening. Even if a company registered a patent for a new fabric, it was almost impossible for a small company to challenge and take on one of the giants in the industry. So Tricosa just kept ahead with the design of new fabrics each season until finally their overheads and costs became too prohibitive to continue. Sadly, they closed their business in the late 1970s.

By the latter part of 1960, advertising and PR suddenly came to the forefront. Due to the success of our first newsletter, we had dipped a finger in by occasionally sending out mailshots to highlight something new; but we were now approached by both an advertising agent and a local P R person. We were aware that with the change in attitudes and the flooding of the market with cheap, badly made clothes, we needed to keep our unique selling points to the forefront. Business either goes forward or backward, it is rarely possible simply to stand still. So we engaged the advertising agent to redesign our formal invitations and programmes for our shows. Until then, fancy invitations were considered non-U—that is, ill bred or plebeian—but we now felt that it was time we broke out from the traditional mould and produced something that was more eye-catching than the conventional.

Our PR was less successful than our new look. We were told that editorial write-ups were of much more value than advertising. We did some photo shoots in one of the Cardington hangars with the airships as a background, plus various other locations around the town. Anglia Television featured us on one occasion, and local magazines and newspapers also took stories occasionally. However, the cost and effort seemed to outweigh the return. Maybe we expected more immediate effect, and perhaps the result could be better seen in the continual increase in our turnover.

Advertising was developed long term, by devising a regular newsletter in the Bedfordshire Times. We took a full-length outside column on the right-hand side of the paper, on one of the early pages alongside editorial. In this way, we avoided getting mixed up with other advertising, and gathered a regular readership as though it was editorial. Every week there was a new story, often linked to current affairs. Originally the unions insisted that one of their members must produce the column. We were willing, but they had no one able to do it in the time. Tuesday night Estelle and I sat up late and burnt the midnight oil. She wrote the column, and I sketched the latest newly arrived stock. We were very proud of this innovative column, which brought success and some instant results each week.

Models talking to a trader at Bedford Market are photographed for publicity.

INVITATION

Our invitations took many forms.

The above was set on a photograph of the woven wool fabric of the winter white dress that Thelma wore when commentating on the show of that season, which was always her role. The dress (now in the Cecil Higgins Collection) was made in the workroom in a simple shift design, all that was needed to show off the very expensive French fabric!

Below is our international "Welcome" design.

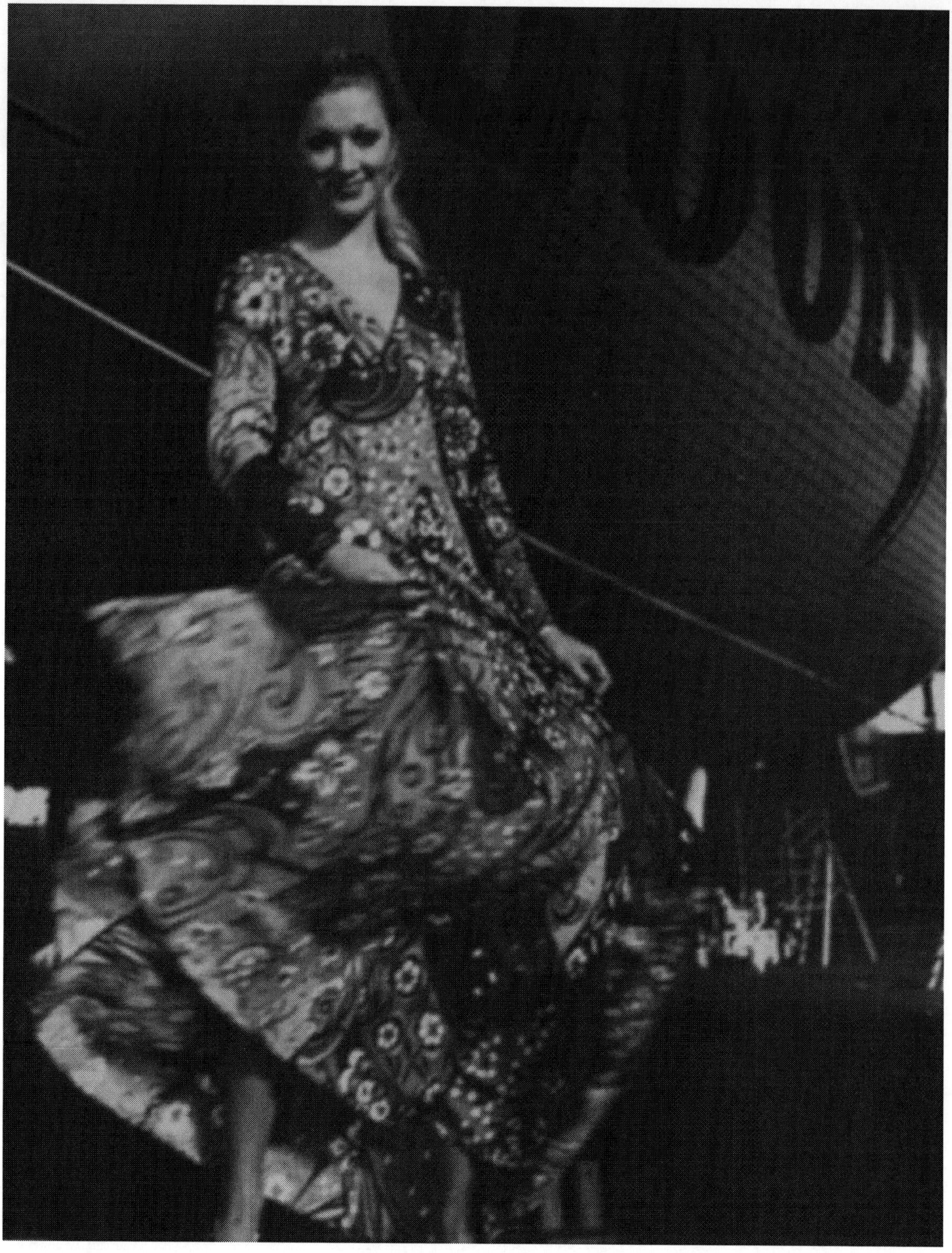

In March 1967, a more sporty image was developed by showing the Spring fashions in conjunction with Marshalls of Cambridge in their showrooms in Goldington Road. During the event both cars and clothes were sold! The programme listed names for oufits such as Convertible, Top Gear, Easy Traveller, Trophy Winner and Hidden Worth. This was another of our PR exercises—but each time we took a collection out of our showroom, we always resolved not to do it again because of the hassle and risk of damage in transporting the clothes. That evening it poured with rain...

In the same year, the Herts & Beds Topic commented on our winter collection in their editorial by saying that PARIS was on the doorstep—*fashion-wise*—in Bedford. Clothes, full of dash and fashion flair with an international flavour, combined with a collection of D'Arcy & Rosamunde's own designs, made for a show worth remembering.

Our imminent entry to the Common Market in 1972 prompted us to have an international theme. Our invitations set the scene, "Welcome" being written in several languages on the cover. International flags blazed the same message in the windows, and Anglia Television visited the show, to feature us later on the Trend programme.

Many of the older customers would come regularly to buy a dress, although they clearly did not need one, just to visit and have a chat. The charade of shortening the length: "Could you please tack it, just in case it is not *quite* the right length," in order to make yet another appointment for a fitting, was often just another outing for a lonely person. We were happy to oblige, as it was all part of our service.

Rosemary, our most photogenic model wearing a fluid line evening gown in the draughty hangars at Cardington. In the background can be seen the Goodyear airship.

Like the hairdresser, we were trusted with many secrets, and provided a listening service for many customers. One of the saddest times was when a customer lost her husband, only to find that everything was in his name and the accounts frozen, rendering her penniless until some arrangements could be made. At one time, other customers had investments, but the income was taxed at 99 pence in the pound, which, unless they could sell the investment, prevented them from purchasing clothes when they needed them.

I think that the fact that we always retained our formality in the showroom, giving each member of staff her title, either Miss or Mrs, maintained the air of professional respect. However, in the workroom there was less formality than in front of the customers, and certainly we had a lot of fun.

Mrs Dowler provided pastoral care in the business, alerting us to any potential problems. Similarly, she could be relied on to sort out problems discreetly whenever possible. It was not until many years later that we learnt that she would often quietly repair "accidental damage" to the children's clothing, when they came home from school or after an outing with her to the park, without ever mentioning it to us.

> Our old mentor Mattie provided us with one piece of valuable advice: you can say almost anything within reason with a kindly smile on your face.

13. Into the 1970s

Easy-care knitted outfits could be dressed up or down to suit the occasion.

On the fashion scene of 1970, the chief topic of conversation was the new "midi" length. Strangely enough, it was the younger woman who dropped her hemline, sometimes right down to the ankle, whilst the older woman preferred to stay with the knee length, as it made her feel younger!

For dinner parties, however, soft full-length woollen gowns gave a romantic feeling to the evening and were an instant success. I still have in my wardrobe from that period two beautiful printed Liberty woollen dresses which are still a joy to wear *and* I do still wear them on occasions.

The race had now really started, and innovation was constantly needed to keep up. There were not many firms like Rogaire, the London agent for the Jacques Heim ready-to-wear collection, who were still manufacturing high-quality merchandise; but we were warned that these garments represented the end of an era, for they were made by Russian Jewish émigré tailors who were about to retire. When that happened, there would be no one to replace them with the necessary skills to continue to make this collection.

Coco Chanel died in 1971. She had retired, but returned to the fashion scene in the 1950s. The Chanel suit bound with braid with an edge-to-edge jacket is her lasting memorial. Her fashion house continued after her death in the same mode until 1983, when Karl Lagerfeld was appointed to capture the new youthful market whilst still retaining the faithful clients.

Following in the mode of Chanel with classic elegant clothes, D'Arcy & Rosamunde presented a major show in 1971 at Hinchingbrooke House near Huntingdon, in aid of the British Red Cross. They swere supported by many of their friends, and fifty advertisers in the printed programme. So many tickets were sold for the event that it was necessary to show the collection in both the library and the ballroom. It was probably the finest presentation that we had ever given, as our wholesalers allowed us to show many Parisian couture models to order, alongside a really beautiful ready-to-wear collection of outfits and evening gowns.

Seven models, Estelle along with Terry, Carmen, Monica, Ann, Jill and Rosie, swirled around with great panache to the strains of romantic music, wearing elegant model daywear and evening gowns with matching shoes supplied by Colton Brothers of Bedford. Afterwards canapés and drinks were served by members of the British Red Cross, and it proved to be a very enjoyable and rewarding evening, raising a sizeable sum for the British Red Cross funds.

As an aside, at this time Bedford was noted for the number of shoe shops in the town, and people came from far and wide to buy their shoes there. It is known in trading circles that two shops selling the same type of merchandise side by side attract more trade than just one outlet on its own. Later we took a concession from a well-known firm in Northampton and sold shoes at No 40 Harpur Street, along with hats, handbags, gloves and jewellery. That then made it possible for a customer to select a complete outfit from tip to toe for a special occasion, all under one roof.

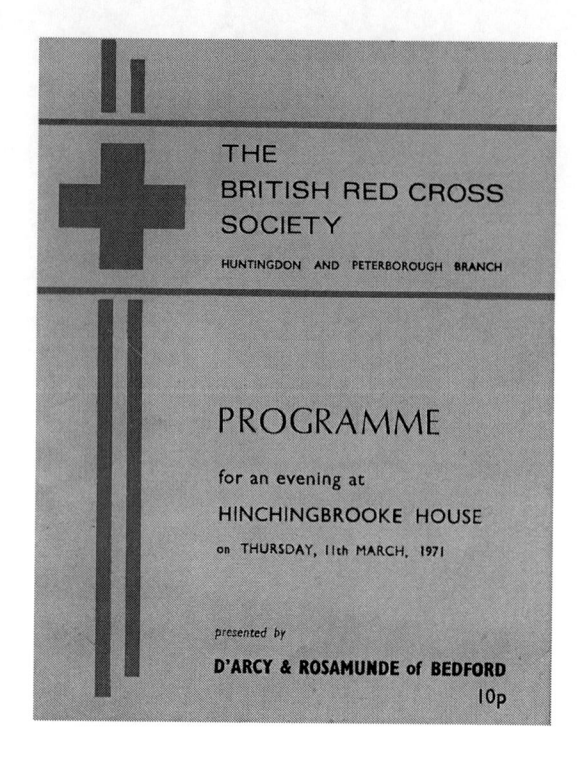

THE BRITISH RED CROSS SOCIETY
HUNTINGDON AND PETERBOROUGH BRANCH

PROGRAMME

for an evening at
HINCHINGBROOKE HOUSE
on THURSDAY, 11th MARCH, 1971

presented by
D'ARCY & ROSAMUNDE of BEDFORD
10p

Why did D'Arcy & Rosamunde support the British Red Cross in Cambridgeshire? Because Lily Eayrs had been a prominent member of the St Neots Branch over many years. Thelma also joined in 1947 and did her basic training in First Aid and Home Nursing there. During the war, Lily served many hours in uniform, doing duty in the operating theatre at Huntingdon Hospital, at Paxton Park Maternity Hospital and receiving the evacuees on their arrival at St Neots. Over the years, she had been a member, she had served as Quartermaster, and both as Commandant of the St Neots Branch and later Area Organiser. In 1988 Lily received her fifty-year British Red Cross long-service medal.

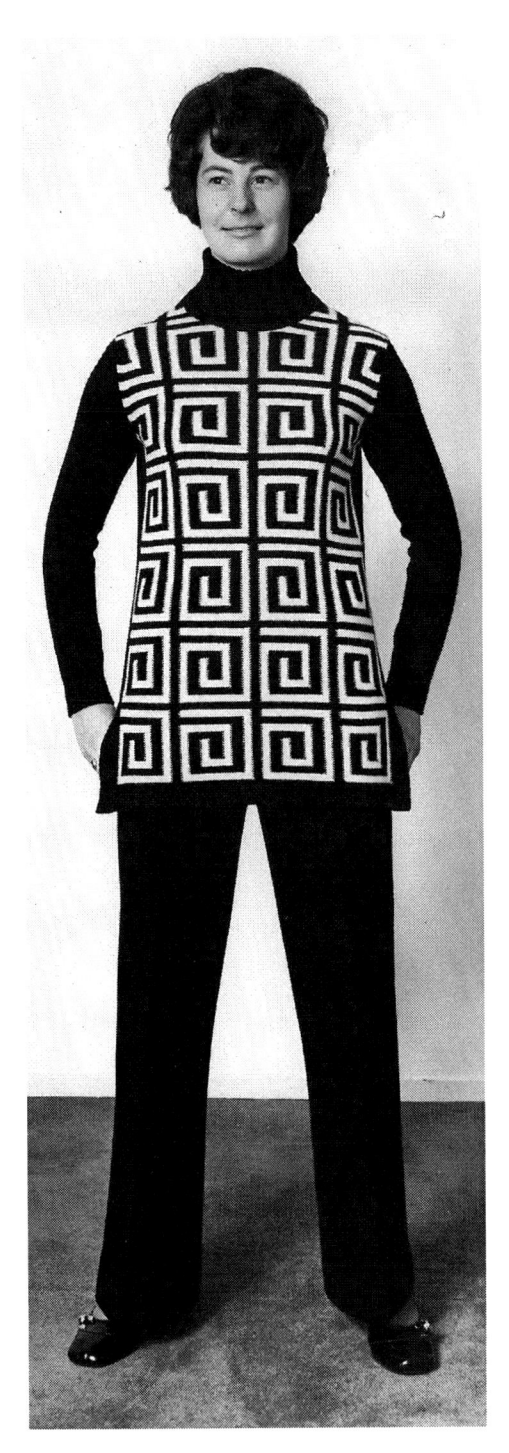

Monica Wilkinson models a Scottish Intarsia knitted trouser suit

The trouser suit for women gradually gained recognition over the period of the 1970s, beginning with wide and flared trousers which gradually narrowed until they were like drain pipes. D'Arcy & Rosamunde did venture into jeans eventually, but only when a stretch "jean" fabric was imported from America and they became comfortable to wear.

In the meantime, all the Far Eastern countries jostled to become involved. The Chinese had the fine sewing skills, and Hong Kong emerged with beautifully beaded conventional evening gowns at ridiculous prices. How could they do it? The answer was simple — cheap labour. Very soon we were told that our Trade Union officials went out to advise and help them raise their wages. Then for a while the entrepreneurs moved to Singapore, then Thailand and eventually Korea, before moving to the Eastern Bloc countries of Europe. If you look at the labels, you will see that this situation is still continuing today and heralds the norm for the future in many manufactured goods. As a result, with their backs to the wall, most manufacturers found it more and more difficult to make clothes in this country, and many went out of business, as indeed many of the cloth manufacturers had done in the earlier decades.

In every direction, choice was diminishing as firms rationalised. It began with the fabric manufacturers who cut down their choice of colours and types of fabric to concentrate on middle-market volume sales. Then in order to buy something a little different or special, the top end became more and more expensive and rare. The design of clothes followed the same pattern, with the bulk sales going into simple shirts, skirts and trousers.

Sports clothes used designer labels to show their difference, rather than necessarily design and quality. Some of the prices that were charged were quite iniquitous. Similarly, the real quality speciality clothing became more and more expensive.

There was one good aspect to this change. The quality in the lower-priced goods stocked by the multiples greatly improved, so that everyone could achieve a reasonable standard of dress with a modest outlay. Careful buying and flair in the assembly could enable the average office girl to look a million dollars. Sadly, some British girls did not share the advantage of the natural fashion flair, with which many of their French counterparts were born.

However, having lived with the wonderful choice and variety of earlier years, I found the changes difficult to accept. Once again, the German firms were first in the field with many quality innovations, showing simple well-cut clothes with colour and design flair. However, unless the whole collection was suitable to buy for your clientele, it was difficult to achieve the numbers in an order to satisfy their usual requirements of a minimum order of, say, two dozen items. The stores could take a dozen each of two winning designs, but it was not possible for us to do that in a small market town.

In spite of difficulties, our turnover consistently increased over the years, helped by write-ups in Vogue *"Shophound"* column and the Draper's Record. These enhanced our national reputation and brought us customers from the north of Scotland to Cornwall, Wales, and not least, Bournemouth, the largest centre for model clothes.

As casual clothes came to the fore, D'Arcy & Rosamunde adopted a more casual approach.

14. Our 25th Anniversary

In 1976, D'Arcy & Rosamunde celebrated their twenty-fifth anniversary in business in Bedford. What enormous changes had been witnessed over the years: from scarcity to haute couture and then high quality to mass production. No longer were any models being designed and made in our own workroom. The remaining seamstresses were fully occupied with the large number of alterations. There were no apprentices in training, and concern was felt that eventually the high standards expected and achieved would no longer be sustainable.

The demise of our apprentice training scheme was due to the Wages Board decree in 1973 that the wages of apprentices should increase rapidly and very steeply, which made training no longer viable. Youngsters were still applying to train, and could not understand that, whilst they were willing to come at a price that could be afforded, by law they could not be employed. So reluctantly and with much sadness, we were obliged to discontinue the training of fifteen-year-olds, as appeals to the Wages Board could not move them.

At a later date, when the consequences of the rapid abandonment of apprenticeships in most industries were being regretted, I wrote the following to The Times newspaper on July 1st 1980, and it was printed as the lead letter in the Business Section:

Sir,
Sir Keith Joseph had suggested that the unemployed should offer their services at lower

than "standard" rates and thereby reduce unemployment, but in many cases when young people are prepared to accept less in order to acquire a skill, employers are prevented, by law, from engaging them at less than that dictated by their Wages Council.

For close on thirty years, I have been a director of a small dress business. In the early years, we designed and made our own collections and had a workroom employing 10 girls, with a much sought after apprenticeship scheme. Seven years ago, the Wages Council raised the wages to such a point that the public would no longer pay the price. We were thus obliged to stop making in the workroom and now import the majority of the goods that we sell from overseas.

The irony of the situation is that since then we have had many applications for apprenticeship from young people who would be prepared to work for an economic wage in order to acquire a skill. They cannot understand why they are prevented from doing so by a Wages Council who appear to take no account of the market situation.

Is it not time that the role of the Wages Council, originally set up with such good intention, should be reviewed in the light of the changing position of this country in its trading relationships with the rest of the world? Surely the time has come for the Wages Council to take a more realistic view of their long term responsibilities. Or, should they indeed have this power to deprive an individual of employment?

Yours faithfully,
Thelma Marks

This letter prompted two replies, one printed on 8th July from the Low Pay Unit and another on 16th July from the General Secretary of the National Union of Tailors and Garment Workers, both focusing on the low wages paid, or the going rate for young people. In subsequent correspondence with them, it became apparent that they felt we should be able to train an apprentice in six weeks! Clearly they equated our business with the wholesale practices of manufacture, where six weeks was the recognised time taken for training an operator to accomplish one operation of manufacture.

Mass production has never appealed to me, despite the fact that, even when I left college in 1948, it was possible to get twice the wage in many roles in wholesale production compared with that in model and bespoke work. The search for quality and beauty in fashion had always consumed me, and I have found it rewarding, albeit very demanding. However, with the advent of the Sixties, the young and not-so-young rebels threw all the established criteria out of the window. Clothes were thrown together to get effect, and there was much talk about the "disposable society". Much hinged on the new-found freedom established for women with the introduction of the contraceptive pill. Socially all was in flux. Eventually I came to understand the situation better after reading the book "Zen and the Art of Motor Cycle Maintenance" by Robert M. Persig. Even though I reached a better understanding, there was still much that I could not accept.

In 1975 STREAKING arrived! At Lord's cricket ground the famous streaker gave a new meaning in fashion to "getting media exposure". At the same time "fashion" began to seem irrelevant,

On the left-hand page, THE TIMES newspaper shows what giant changes can take place in quite a short period of history.

as the media focused on the regular famines in Ethiopia, starvation in Bangladesh and other problems around the world.

My Christian faith had been steadily growing as the building blocks of the business began to crumble, and I questioned my role in the business. I also found it difficult to maintain my enthusiasm. After the mid-1970s, buying became much more difficult as the breadth and depth of the merchandise diminished. Without our own designs being made in the workroom, we felt it was necessary to advertise, which we did by taking a weekly column in the Bedfordshire Times.

1981 saw the wedding of the Prince of Wales and Lady Diana Spencer. The customer who applauded us at our first show came in to the showroom to express her disgust. "How could the bride have been allowed to arrive with a crumpled train - *and* the bodice of the dress did not fit? You would not have allowed a bride out like that," she said. "Obviously no one had shown the Princess how to sit and arrange the wedding gown in the carriage." Both of these criticisms were true, for we always had a practice session on how to arrange the dress in the car and how to kneel, etc.

To compensate we fell back on to the old French adage in the fashion trade, which says that, with a collection of fine belts and scarves, it is possible to manage with a minimal classic wardrobe of clothes. This is providing that the basic clothes are in a plain neutral colour (preferably beige, navy or black).

So we increased our range of accessories and bought as many plain-coloured outfits as possible.

A one-sized pleated evening gown from Hawaii- both of

15. First principles

Having broken bones in both sides of one ankle and had cartilage removed from both knees—once as a result of skiing, the other from catching a stiletto heel between paving stones in the Louvre— I have visited the physiotherapist on many occasions. The physio will always tell you that pointed-toe shoes damage your feet. The pointed toe pulls the big toe in and causes the joint to swell and form a bunion in later life. So as soon as I left the fashion business I resolved never to wear pointed shoes again. Fortunately I was able to stock up with shoes when square toes were in vogue for a while, and I am utterly amazed that the shoe designers have not taken this aspect on board generally.

As a result, I have also said to customers on many occasions: "If your feet are uncomfortable, it will show on your face, so buy some comfortable and elegant shoes before shopping for your outfit." Often hats were chosen in advance as well, because the framing of the face for the photographs is of vital importance. Once those decisions were made, it was usually simple to complete the design with a bespoke outfit if something ready-made was not available.

Building a wardrobe was a constant theme at D'Arcy & Rosamunde over all the years. Customers appreciated the thought and care that we took to ensure that they avoided white elephants amongst their ensembles. About this time the "layered" look first appeared, along with the practical ability to cope with different climates and temperature. I recall particular customers whose husbands were elected to national bodies, which entailed travelling all over the world. Fitting them out with

these gowns uncrushable and ideal for travelling.

a minimum travel wardrobe for all occasions that mixed and matched was one of our specialities. These were favourite commissions which were very rewarding.

Easy-care, uncrushable fabrics were a boon, but they came at a price. The research that enabled this advance must be appreciated; but, that said, it was not a universal success story. The early advent of nylon jumps to mind immediately. It was hot and smelly to wear, although the ultimate easy-care fabric. Medically it also caused trouble. Women particularly suffered from thrush through wearing nylon tights in the days before the cotton gusset was inserted. Nylon was also very static and attracted the dirt. Crimplene followed nylon, and this fabric enjoyed a great period of popularity, but it was bulky and had its faults. So gradually, the synthetic yarn was added to other fibres to produce the mixtures of fabric that we enjoy today. Even now, there is a school of thought that believes that the natural fibres are the most healthy to wear. Certainly I prefer the very fine Sea Island cotton to wear in very hot climates, to any of the other breathable materials that are promoted.

Today we also take comfort for granted. It would be difficult to move back to rigid structures of the Jean Patou tailoring of the 1970s. Only the military, like the Guards in ceremonial gear, still wear the heavy structured tailoring of the past. For everyday wear, even the forces now opt for comfort and practicability.

As you look into the L'Officiel magazines that were preserved by D'Arcy & Rosamunde, you will notice that many of the illustrations from the early magazines have been torn out. This is because

An early L'Officiel of 1947, the cover of which is illustrated by the most famous of the fashion artists, Gruau, whose signature can be recognised with a star, in the bottom corner.

these were real workhorses of the fashion industry, and after the restrictions of utility labelling and rationing by coupons, many designs were greedily torn out to be copied.

These magazines also were very expensive to buy in their day. Their layouts were produced with hand lettering by artists, and they contained wonderful photography before the ease of computer-aided design. So they really represented the best of that era.

You may also notice that in 1974 L'Officiel magazine was cut down in size, although it has been bound in the same size cover for uniformity. In the 1970s, like Vogue, L'Officiel deviated from just fashion in clothing to include fashion in architecture and other allied disciplines, along with sport and other interests. They also padded the magazine out with more and more advertising. So D'Arcy & Rosamunde cut down on the expense and bought only the first issue of the season with the shows in it. Even that became an irrelevance, as many of the clothes in the Paris shows were not suitable for the average woman.

Ethnic fashions filled the gap for many people. They were first worn by the hippies in the 1960s, who rejected consumerism and wore them in their own individual way-out styles. Paris picked up the theme, producing peasant-style dresses. Here, Laura Ashley began to make simple cotton dresses in a peasant/Kate Greenaway style. When they first appeared on the market, they looked as though they had been made by a home dressmaker, and were incredibly cheap. The young seized on the pretty styles. As a result, she became very successful and grew very quickly. As she did so, her quality and her prices increased, and she gained a very respected position, particularly with soft furnishing and house decoration that reflected her fashion style.

In the mid-1970s some of the most way-out young appeared on the streets in punk fashions Their styles consciously sought to shock. The key figure in the punk movement was Vivienne Westwood. Although we had the tradition of showing some crazy ensembles in our shows to create some laughter and fun, we did not stretch to the way-out and weird that was espoused by Vivienne towards the end of the 1970s. A very talented designer, she epitomised the outrageous mode in the whole of her collection. It certainly caught the eye of the press, but to our way of thinking, good taste had been thrown to the wind at the altar of sex, in order to gain publicity. But on the principle that fashion reflects the social mode, maybe she was reflecting what was happening in society generally. Historically it had happened before, notably in the 1820s, when girls wore simple see-through muslin dresses and damped them to hug and show off their figures.

Again in the 1920s, after a long period of modesty in the Victorian era, woman had shortened their dresses and flattened their bosoms to show off their independence. In each of these cases, the pendulum swung eventually, so maybe it will happen again soon. My own prediction is that it will come with the eventual disillusionment of woman's supposed liberation. The realization may come that men and women are different and that the difference needs to be respected. I have never felt any disadvantages in being a woman, and have always celebrated my femininity. When my sister and I started our careers in the fashion industry,

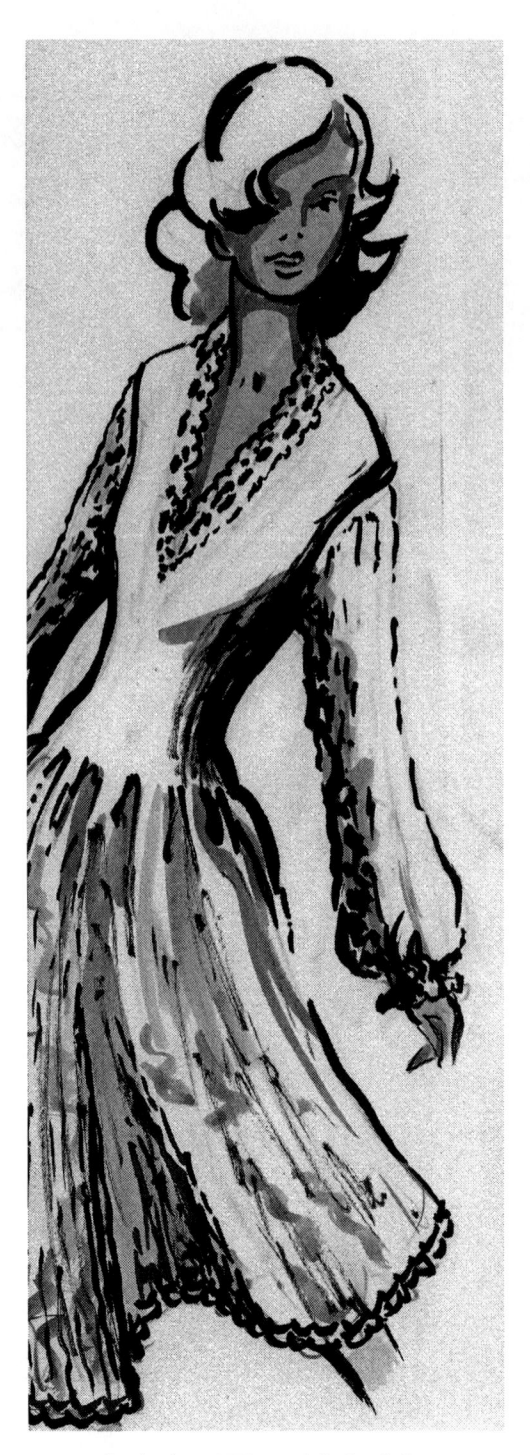

In the late 1970s, soft knitted dresses and two-pieces were very popular -

and flattering for the figure.

many people feared for us with our inexperience in a highly volatile industry, especially as we were two young girls.

However, I cannot remember any occasion when we were at a disadvantage because we were girls. I have to say that we were never in business for the money. Our only concern was to balance the budget, but generally we never worried about it. Just occasionally, natural human friction caused some agitation, but not for long. In buying generally, I was blessed with a natural intuition for the next trend, and always abandoned a style before it had completed its run, in favour of something new. In this way we were rarely left with out-of-date stock.

Towards the end of the 1970s, a representative called into the showroom and asked if he could show us a range of hand-knitted dresses from Spain. This seemed to me to be going too far, but Estelle had seen one of these dresses being worn, and immediately agreed. How pleased I was that she was there, as we were grateful to have such an easy and malleable look to sell for special occasions. These dresses were incredibly flattering and needed no alterations. The colours were so soft and pretty that anyone could wear them, even the largest sizes. It was a look that lasted for about three summers, and then was over-exploited and died.

After the mid-1970s the 25-year fashion cycle had gone around, and I was beginning to lose my relish for the buying. Everyone was rationalising and there was a narrowing of choice, particularly in fabrics. Looking at the Tricosa brochures, I can now see that I was not alone. The traditional fashion scene did not know where to go. Sports clothes were the only growth area, as the American idea of casual dressing crept in on us.

So Estelle joined me and took a larger part in the decision-making of the buying. We discussed my feelings and considered the options. Since the arrival of the children, time only allowed me to sketch fashions. Now I was hankering towards painting again; but when you are in the position of employing others and own a business, you cannot hand in your notice, even though without the designing and making of our own collection, the business now no longer depended on me.

Monica, my right hand in the business, married in 1972 and went to live in Hunstanton. I missed her very much. Mrs Dowler and Ann, our last apprentice, were then trained to do simple fittings. As a necessity, alterations were now restricted to shortening hems and minor adjustments.

Photographed at the home of Thelma Marks

16. The Easter Burglary

By 1980, there only remained about four years on our long twenty-year lease, last negotiated in 1964. Rents had zoomed up over that time, and we had been unable to buy the property. This made it difficult to sell the business, although at intervals we had made enquiries into the possibility.

When we confided in one of our wholesaler friends that we would like to sell the business, he mentioned that he might know of someone who could be interested. In due course a meeting was arranged with the interested party, and negotiations started in the spring of 1982.

In the meantime, towards the end of March, a telephone call from the police at about half-past midnight summoned me to the business as the alarm was sounding. I duly drove into Bedford, by which time the alarm had stopped. However, I was directed to lead the police into the premises so that they could ensure that no one had broken in. Strange but true, on such occasions the owner must go in first, and I was followed by a policewoman and then a policeman. I just hoped that no one was there, as we did not seem very formidable, should we come face to face with a robber. However, all was well — it was a false alarm. So I locked up and went home.

On the following Saturday night, which was the Easter weekend, there was another call from the police. This time the alarm was not sounding, but a constable on the beat had noticed that the back gate was open and swinging in the breeze. I asked him if he would check the premises, and he reported back that all the doors and windows

Knitted easy-care fabrics in beautiful colours took on a formal air. Worn with smart accessories they were ideal for weddings and special occasions, but nevertheless could come into service in an everyday capacity.

were locked and all seemed well except for the gate. I said that, since it was a rickety old gate, it could wait until the morning, and so I did not turn out to investigate.

In the middle of the following Easter Sunday night, there was another telephone call from the police, asking me to come into Bedford. A person walking his dog had noticed someone trying to enter our premises, had alerted the police, and they had caught a man.

I was feeling well pleased with the police, and arrived to find a number of them with a dog. Again I opened up and led the party into the premises. All was well in the workroom, where the intruder was caught trying to enter, so I then opened the security door to the showroom and put on the light. I gasped and could not believe my eyes! The showroom was empty, with the exception of a few garments that could be seen from the street outside, and the display pinned to the walls.

Should I laugh or should I cry? I was dumbstruck. A few black dustbin-liners were left on the floor, otherwise everywhere was tidy. Two bars had been broken in a small back window and the window lock was broken. Somehow or other the thieves appeared to have neutralised the alarm.

The police got some of the story from the Sunday night intruder. The thieves had taken the stock in a hire van across from Harwich to the Hook of Holland with all the Easter holidaymakers and it was never to be seen again. As the raid had been so successful, on his way back the intruder had decided to try to get into the workroom area where all the leather bags and shoes were stored. He had not bargained for pre-war installed metal bars, which were much tougher than the post-war ones at the back of the showroom. He dared not grass on his accomplices, as he said that he had a wife and children to consider. So he went to prison. Eventually, after two years, we received a letter from Thames Valley police to thank us for our help and say that the instigator of the crime had been caught. He was a prominent member of one of the London councils, who had a gang of heavies around him to organise the jobs and then burglars to do them. As well as our burglary, a warehouse in the east end of London had been burgled on the same night.

There were panic stations for a week. The stock was insured but not the loss of profit, and there were wages and overheads to be paid. So whilst Estelle attended to the insurance claim, I dashed to London to find some stock to carry us over until the end of the season when new stock would be arriving. Our wholesaler friends were very good, taking one or two outfits from the large store orders, and thus we managed to get through the season.

With only a small amount of stock, the business was much easier to sell. The prospective buyer eventually agreed a price, and the business was sold later that year. In many ways it was a sad day for us, but it was a matter of great relief that the new owner appreciated the staff and treated them very well. None of them lost their jobs. When the lease was up for renewal, the business was moved to new premises in Dame Alice Street, where they continued to trade until 1999.

To everything there is a season, a time to every purpose.   Ecclesiastes 3.1

A classic wedding outfit in pure wool worsted that was sold in a multitude of beautiful art shades.

17. The Collection

When the business was sold, the old L'Officiel magazines which I had hoarded year by year, were collected from the cellar and brought home. The pile was very heavy and consisted of some hundreds of glossy magazines. They had sat in the back of the shop until the pile became too large. Then they had been relegated into the cellar. I could not bear to part with them, as they were a part of my life. What was I going to do with them now? It took me almost twenty years to decide.

Whilst visiting the famous Costume Museum in Bath, I had noticed that they had a collection of L'Officiel amongst their treasures. My mind then focused on the Cecil Higgins Art Gallery. Might they welcome them, as they were an authoritative record of fashion over the years from 1951 to 1982? A visit from Caroline Bacon, the curator, confirmed that indeed they would like them. I also showed her many of the clothes that I had kept because they represented never-to-be-repeated fabrics and workmanship. She told me of the wonderful collection of historic fashion from over the ages, hidden away in the archives of the Museum, and told me of her dream to have a specially designed gallery in which to show them eventually.

I agreed to leave the magazines to the Cecil Higgins Art Gallery in my will. Shortly afterwards, Caroline asked to borrow some for an exhibition, and to my horror, when I opened one of them, I found that the binding had rotted and the pages cascaded out. Not all of them were numbered, so I needed my rusting French to determine the order by reading the copy. Something had to be done.

I was lucky in finding John Lawrence, a superb bookbinder working away in his garage, who came to my rescue. I designed a cover of green and gold, and he bound them beautifully into seasons — Autumn and Spring of each year.

Next it seemed sensible to catalogue all the clothes, so that the family would know which items were promised to the Cecil Higgins Art Gallery after my death. As I described each garment, I dwelt back in the period, and incidents and cameos flooded back into my mind. What fun I had, walking down memory lane! Caroline read some of the comments and asked me to record as many memories as possible. So this small book evolved. It is dedicated to all those who ever worked with us at D'Arcy & Rosamunde and contributed to the ethos which was our business. Some names have been mentioned in the text, but regardless of that, everyone— all of the customers and all of the staff were equally important.

Many people have also asked us: "Are you going to leave your fashion collection to your grandchildren?" To which I answer: "Our clothes collection needs to be cared for in a way that the modern generation would not have the knowledge and experience to do, so they need to have professional care. For this reason, Estelle and I have sadly parted with most of our treasures in the hope that they will be cared for in a way that makes them available for future generations to see and appreciate."

After some consideration, both Estelle and I decided that the collection should pass to the Cecil Higgins Art Gallery in our lifetime, rather than after we die. This decision can probably be traced back to my father, who told us not to expect anything when he died, as he was giving us all that he could afford in his lifetime. In that way, he could share in our pleasure. The purchase of a business for us at the ages of eighteen and twenty-one was certainly evidence of his philosophy, and gave not only him, but many other people, great pleasure as well.

Regrettably, we were so busy paying our way in the 1950s that we did not keep many records of that period. In any case, photography was very expensive at that time, and I only owned a basic Brownie box camera. The photograph on page 24 was taken by our neighbour with that camera in her garden at her insistence. However, when one looks back back, it is quite daunting suddenly to realise that a large part of your life has now been relegated to the history books.

opposite page...
Rosemary models a timeless trouser suit, made of washable jersey from Switzerland, in the Cardington hangar in front of the Goodyear airship

---

The L'Officiel magazines (1951-1982)
and the D'Arcy & Rosamunde Collection
can be seen by appointment at
The Cecil Higgins Art Gallery in Bedford

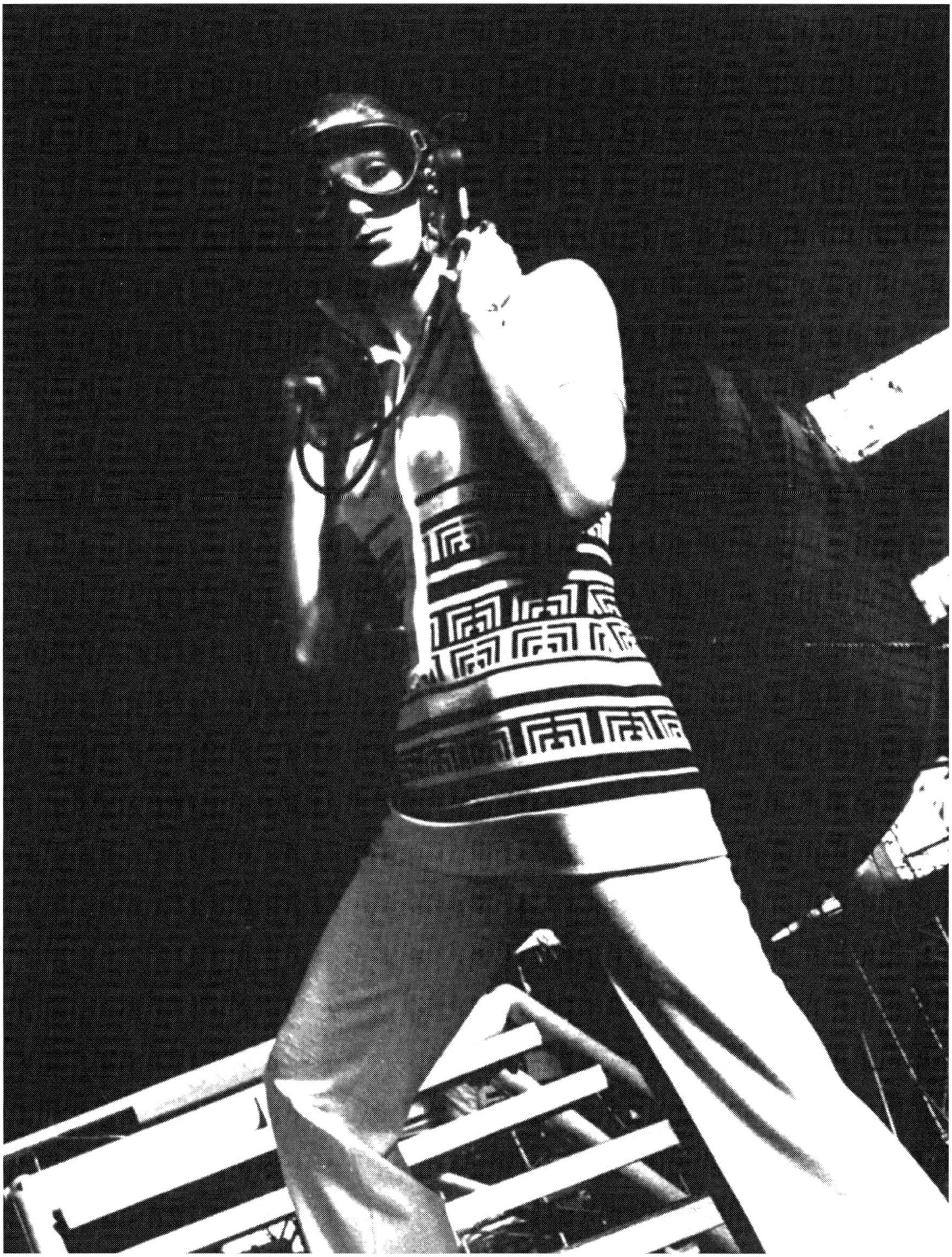

Estelle Addington nee Eayrs.

18. Estelle's Footnote

✿ We were privileged to do what we did.

✿ Father showed great faith in us at a young age.

✿ Mother gave us her unfailing support.

✿ Dear Mattie was a guiding light.

✿ In the early days, we handled the most beautiful fabrics, now no longer available.

✿ Our workroom consisted of the tailoress and many seamstresses, who over the years were trained by Thelma, and gained the experience to make up her original designs.

✿ The majority of our staff stayed with us for many years, giving us stability and their loyal support.

✿ There would have been no business without our excellent vendeuses.

✿ We had the support of many loyal clients.

✿ I had some superb clothes because of my shape — always a good coat hanger!

✿ The early years were the most uplifting— but, financially, not so rewarding as selling the ready-to-wear collections.

✿ We had a lot of fun, but I am relieved to be out of the rag trade.

✿ Fabrics, finish and choice leave much to be desired today.

19. Some Staff Comments

Wanda says:

✿ It was a family-run business which was quite different from the relationship with a manager or manageress.

✿ We were surrounded by lovely things.

✿ Miss Jefferson, a rather old-fashioned lady who cooked for us in the basement, made it seem just like Upstairs - Downstairs.

✿ The atmosphere was lovely,—so personal and so warming. And the reason why?

✿The family—especially Mrs Eayrs—looked after us personally.

Monica says:

✿ Travelling from Luton to Bedford by train— to D'Arcy & Rosamunde took three hours out of my day, but I always looked forward to a varied and interesting work schedule when I arrived.

✿ Creating a garment from the first consultation with the customer, purchasing the material which was invariably an elaborately embroidered or beaded silk or satin from London's West End, to final fitting when the outfit was completed, gave satisfaction which was well rewarded by the pleasure of the client.

✿ One of my most lasting memories of the thirteen-years spent at D'Arcy & Rosamunde is of the annual Spring and Autumn fashion shows. Many working hours led to a united feeling within the staff of the workroom and showroom, creating an occasion that would always be more successful than the previous time.

✿ Without the enthusiasm of Mrs Marks and Mrs Addington to develop the business as they did, I should truly have missed out on an experience of a lifetime.

Wanda Eames (Philcox) née Fantuz

Monica Richardson née Wilkinson

Joan Craddock née Burgoine

✿ When D'Arcy & Rosamunde finally finished training and gave up bespoke tailoring and dressmaking, many of their customers came to me.

✿ I and they appreciated what I had learnt in my training. As a result, it has enabled me to run a business on my own over the past thirty-nine years.

✿ My talent was recognised and, whilst design and dressmaking has never been a well paid occupation, it has given me much satisfaction.

Joan says:

✿ I started to work at D'Arcy & Rosamunde on the 5th January 1958, when I was fifteen years old. I could not have had a better training anywhere. Everything had to be done in the proper way, and if it was not right it had to be unpicked! Even today, I still do not cut corners, as it is quicker in the long term to follow the rules that I learnt in my apprenticeship than to break them.

✿ After about three years, I had some relationship problems within the workroom, but Mrs Marks sorted them out. She encouraged each of us within our capabilities and was respected as a boss. One day, she came in the workroom and saw that a curtain had been hung over one of the doors. "That must be Joan," she said. (Joan had got her husband to fix it for her so as to exclude a draught!)

✿ We all had a lot of fun, but were expected to do a good day's work. Mrs. Eayrs used to say that I was the only one in the workroom who could talk and work! She also used to tell me off for sitting on those lovely hot storage heaters. "You will get piles when you are older," she would say.

✿ There were also rigid rules. No food, drink or smoking were allowed anywhere in the workroom or showroom, to avoid damage to the clothes. We were lucky to be able to buy a lunch in the basement for 2s. 6d. My mother paid this each week. Other costs were 50 pence for my weekly travel ticket, 50 pence for clothes and my mother encouraged me to save 50 pence.

✿ Travelling to work from Lidlington to St. John's station, meant that I had to leave at 7.15am. It was a long day. At the end of five years, I felt that I had learnt enough to start up on my own. I had had six months working under Miss Faulkner, who gave me the opportunity to learn the essence of tailoring. I had learnt the finer points of couture dressmaking, such as to appliqué lace rather than stitch darts or seams. So by then, I felt that there was not much that I couldn't do. Even then after I had left, I still came back, for a week or so each season, to help at the fashion shows, and would always readily give a hand in an emergency. When I returned, it seemed like coming back home.

21 Some statistics

In 1958 - our tailoress earned £6.0s.0d. per week
and paid 4 shillings tax,

the skilled dressmakers earned £5.10s.0d.
and paid 3 shillings tax

- the apprentice started at £2.5s.10d.

In the 1950s, increments of five to ten shillings a year were normal, but apprentices were given more frequent increases according to the rate of their development over two years of training.

By 1964 - the minimum wages for dressmakers for a 42-hour week were:

1st	6 months of training	1s 3¾d per hour
2nd	6 months of training	1s. 5d per hour
2nd	year of training	1s. 10½d per hour
3rd	year as an improver	2s. 1½d per hour
All other workers		2s.9d per hour
3 years	plus 2 years	2s.11½d per hour

By 1968 - the minimum wages for dressmakers for a 40-hour week were:

1st year - £3. 18s. 4d. per week
2nd year - £5. 4s. 2d. per week
Next 6 months - £5. 16s. 8d per week
All other workers - £7 10s. 0d. per week

By 1971 - our skilled dressmakers earned £11.50 per week and paid £1.05 tax & 88p insurance

Between 1951 and 1982 the number of staff working in the workroom varied between six and ten.

The maximum number of staff working in the business at any one time was 15, which included a part-time cook, a shopper and a cleaner.

20 The Process of Couture—

Design & dressmaking *as practised by D'Arcy & Rosamunde of Bedford*

In the 1950s, Thelma Marks (née Eayrs) was the designer at D'Arcy & Rosamunde. In the 1960s, after the birth of Thelma's children, Monica Wilkinson took over the role. Their aim when designing was client-oriented, rather than imposing their vision. First, they sought to discover any dreams and aspirations and then their challenge was to lead the client in a direction that would enable those dreams to be fulfilled. Largely they were successful, but, whilst preferring to be involved in the selection of the material, inevitably there was the rare occasion when someone brought in a piece of their own material which caused trouble. (See page 30.)

With fabric in hand, it was draped up against the client. How often some subtle nuance would be found that called for a deviation from the original ideas in order to make the best use of the fabric! Maybe it would be a glisten on the cross or a pronounced colour would show in the one way of the fabric.

Once the design was finally agreed, the measurements were then taken. They were:

bust — waist — hips (the widest part)
across the back — across the front
shoulder to waist at the front
shoulder to centre of bust
centre back — neck to waist
length of sleeve from wrist (over elbow with a bent arm) to shoulder - wrist to under arm
round upper arm — lower arm and wrist
shirt length (back and front)
inside and outside leg length for trousers
around thigh and calf

Pattern making came in two forms. Simple designs for skirts and trousers were made on the flat to measurement, whilst more intricate designs were modelled or draped onto a stand. There was a range of different size stands in the workroom and the nearest size was padded out to the customer's measurements. Then the design was interpreted in mull or just occasionally, the actual material.

Mull is a very fine cotton which is used for pattern making. The pattern shape was marked with a pencil line and then the mull was tacked up for a fitting. As time went by, it was found that, providing it was of a suitable texture, the lining could be used for this purpose. The design was then marked on to the lining with a tracing wheel, before being tacked up for the first fitting. In this way the design could be developed to overcome any fitting problems before the fabric was cut. Although very adequate measurements were taken, often it was impossible to determine the occasional stance of a person or an irregular shape. Nothing was set in stone until after the first fitting. Little cost was involved should there be a change of mind or a development that would improve the final garment. Many of the fabrics that were used were very costly so, by using this method, errors were eradicated.

If everyone was happy, then the mull pattern was unpicked and laid out onto the fabric for cutting. It was vital to make sure that the selvedge and grain of the material were placed together at right angles. Often as much as four or five inches was lost as a result of the fabric being cut 'off the grain' when purchased. If the grain **was** twisted, (as could happen), the garment would never sit straight and the skirt would always tend to twist!

After the first fitting, when the fitted lining or mull had been laid onto the fabric and cut out, the lines were pinned through to the other side. They were then **trace tacked** onto each side of the fabric. (see sketch on page 115)

It was often necessary to fit each side of the body individually as one side could differ quite considerably from the other. A physically active person could develop on one side or the other to a greater degree by as much as one and a half inches.

This is where balance marks were invaluable. Many of them were used as it enabled the fabric to be eased in and moulded to fit well on an awkward shape.

The lining was then stitched and pressed. However, the top fabric was **only tacked**, because, if the fabric was thick, it might still need a small amount to be released in order to accommodate any bulk. Alternatively, the fabric might move in a **slightly** different way from the pattern, so that some adjustment might be required. Determining these factors was a matter of experience. After the second fitting the alterations were individually marked once again, by trace tacking with a different coloured tacking thread.

The garment was then tacked up in **matching sylko** because after being stitched it is sometimes very difficult to remove the tacking thread. The removal of all of the tacking thread needed to be done with great care, as the fabric could easily be cut or torn. Most of the marking tacks were removed before the final stitching. All the marking was done with a special tacking thread, which broke very easily. Regrettably it is no longer available.

After the second fitting, each seam was stitched and pressed as the garment was finally made. The order in which each part was made was vital for its construction, as was the pressing. All pressing should be done during construction, so that little further pressing would be needed, except for the hem, when finally the garment was finished.

Tailoring was a slightly different process, as the whole fabric was shrunk before starting! All of the interfacings were also wetted thoroughly, so as to shrink them too. Lots of hissing and steam were involved. Miss Faulkner used traditional tailor tacking and chalk to mark up the pattern in the first instant. However, I did not trust these methods, so in order to ensure accuracy after the first fitting, the garments were trace tacked before the subsequent fittings.

Wedding gowns were made in the last six weeks before a wedding and not finished until a week before the event. At the final fitting, ten days before the event, the bride's anxiety usually made it necessary for the dress to be taken in because of her loss of weight.

Wedding gowns were always wrapped in a sheet and the light kept from them as much as possible, for a white fabric could become cream within that six weeks if exposed to strong light. This also applied to the fading of some other fabrics, so, for protection, every garment was kept in a wrapper made of unbleached calico and hung on thickly padded coat hangers.

I was pleased to see that in museum conservation the same unbleached calico is still used to preserve and keep light off the garments, in order to protect them. So in one respect nothing has changed, and fashion continues to go round in circles.

Bibliography

Costume and Fashion by James Laver
published by Thames and Hudson - Fourth edition 2002.

A History of Fashion by J. Anderson Black & Madge Garland
published Orbis Publishing Limited 1975;
re-issued by Macdonald & Co (Publishers) Ltd 1990.

D'Arcy & Rosamunde Ltd., Wage books — deposited at the Cecil Higgins Art Gallery

A Glossary of Terms

Alcantara, *a synthetic suede resulting from a discovery on an early space mission. The fabric had to be made in a vacuum and the manufacturing of it proved to be very toxic. Later banned so it was redesigned as 'Ultrasuede'.*

Alpaca, *the fine silken-type wool of the South American alpaca, produces a brushed luxury fabric of great softness, usually in a caramel colour*

Angora, *cloth made from the long silky wool of the Anatolian goat, (the true mohair), or from the angora rabbit hair*

Appliqué, *work applied to, or laid on another material*

Balance marks, *tack marks put at right angles across the trace tacking marks, to indicate the position for the joining together of seams*

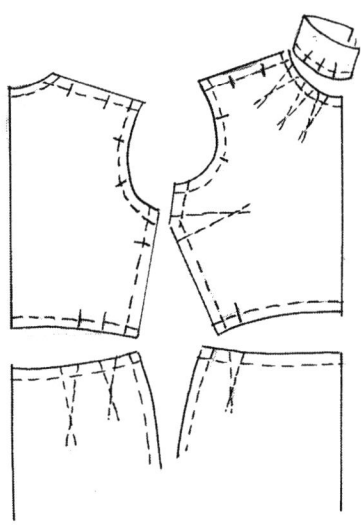

Barathea, *a soft fabric of worsted wool, or wool and silk etc.*

Baste, *to tack when sewing*

Batiste, *a fine fabric of cotton, linen or wool— in French: cambric*

Bias, *fabric cut exactly on the cross. If it is just slightly off the cross, the fabric will twist*

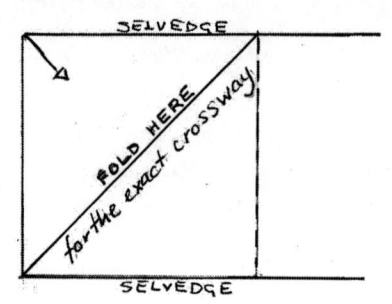

Binding, *additional fabric which is stitched onto an edge, wrapped over, and stitched on the other side*

Bishop sleeve, *a full sleeve caught into the wrist with a cuff, as worn by a bishop*

Blind hem, *a hem that has been added but is invisible*

Boning, *encasing whale-bone, metal or plastic into a tape to stiffen and hold firm*

Bouclé, *a yarn having the threads looped to give bulky effect, can be knitted or woven*

Box pleat, *two pleats facing outwards*

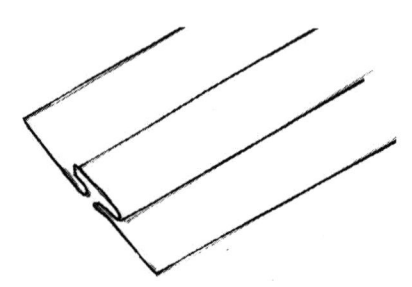

Braid, *originally a plait, then used as an edging or binding, or to outline*

Brocade, *a raised patterned fabric made on a jacquard loom*

Broderie anglaise, *a fine cotton fabric embroidered in a satin stitch with a cut out design of eyelet holes*

Button hole, *there are three types of button hole:*
(1) 'Bound', *when a crossway oblong of fabric is placed on the buttonhole position, then stitched and turned out. The turnings are either opened out or left together facing into the hole. The fabric then binds the buttonhole.*

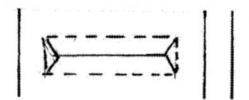

(2) 'Piped', *as before but the tunings are turned away from the centre of the buttonhole to give a piped finish*

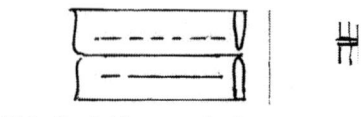

(3) *a* 'Worked' *buttonhole*

of which there are three shapes

Calico, *cotton cloth first brought from Calicut in India: plain white unprinted cotton cloth, bleached or unbleached; or coarse printed cloth*

Cross cut collar velvet, *an expensive, narrow width, closely-woven silk velvet, that was sold in strips on the cross. just for making collars*

Cap sleeve, *the fabric of the bodice extending over the top of the arm to form a sleeve for the top of the arm*

Collar canvas, *a stiff closely-woven canvas that is cut on the cross, in order to stretch it to shape, to fit around the back of the neck*

Facing, *a shaped piece of fabric that is placed on top of an armhole, neck or such like, to stitch around and neatly turn it out to the shape*

Camel hair, *the hair of the camel, used to make a sporty type of coat*
Camisole, *an under bodice*
Cashmere, *the most luxurious hair from the Kashmir goat. Always in short supply, it is very expensive and can be either knitted or woven*
Challis, *a fine matt worsted material*
Chiffon, *a gossamer fine fabric of pure silk or synthetic yarn*
Crepe, *a crimped fabric*
Dolman sleeve, *is cut all in one with the bodice, which gives draped line to the underarm*

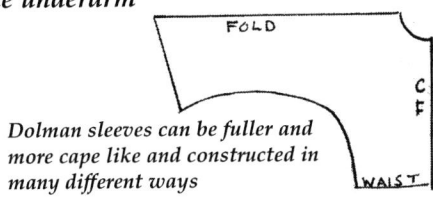

Dolman sleeves can be fuller and more cape like and constructed in many different ways

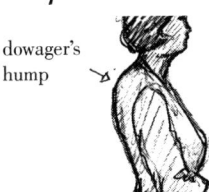

Donegal, *a fine tweed with slubs of a darker or brighter colour*
Dowager's hump *a hump at the back of the neck which elderly people develop as a result of drooping the shoulders. It is difficult to fit*
Eyelet hole, *a punched hole*
Faggoting, *a kind of embroidery in which some of the cross threads are drawn together in the middle and/ or adding strips of rouleau with a decorative stitch*
Faille *a closely-woven silk or rayon fabric with transverse ribs*
Fell *to stitch down with an over turned edge, i.e. usually a lining is felled to the heavier fabric*

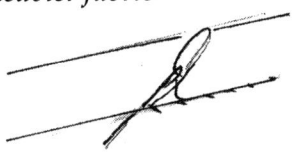

Flat pleat, *pleats that are pressed down flat as opposed to unpressed pleats which are folds without pressing*
French chalk, *a very fine chalk that was used to clean delicate fabrics*
Fly Running, *a fine-running stitch where the needle is held still and pressed gently against the side of the finger, whilst the fabric is oscillated up and down to form the stitch*
Foulard, *a soft twill weave of pure silk or synthetic yarn used mainly for making scarves*
French modelling, *the design of the gown is draped up onto a model and interpreted onto mull fabric to make the pattern*

With experience sometimes the actual fabric may be used to create the design of the garment

French seam, *a narrow seam is first stitched on the right side, pressed open and the stitched again on the wrong side in order to trap the turnings inside the seam. Used only on fine fabrics*

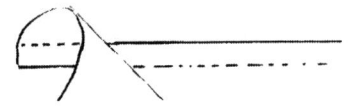

Frogging, *the working of ornamental fastenings and braid trimming often used on the front of uniforms*
Gather, *a running stitch or loose machine stitch that is pulled up to create puckers*

Gores, *triangulars sections that are inserted to give fullness*

Gros-grain, *a heavy corded silk which is mostly used for ribbon and hat bands*

Gusset, *an angular piece of fabric that is inserted to strengthen, enlarge or increase movement in a garment*

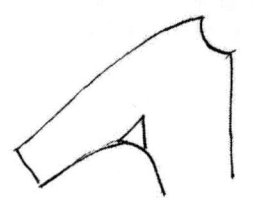

Hair canvas, *a hairy, loosely-woven canvas that is used down the front of a jacket or coat*

Harris tweed, *a thick rough tweed from Scotland*

Hat elastic, *a very fine roll elastic used for putting under the hair to secure a hat*

Hat pins, *long pins with fancy ends that were used to pin the hat to the hair*

Haute couture, *garments made to measure with the highest craftmanship but originally a name given only to the French fashion houses*

Hem, *a folded border of cloth*

Hemstitch, *the hem is folded to a line. Weft threads are then drawn out of the linen at the point of stitching. Whilst hemming, the warp thread are then stitched together in fours and again stitched similarly on the opposite side, which thus creates a series of holes*

Herring bone stitch, *an alternating diagonal stitch, usually used for hems; the stitch allows the fabric to stretch*

Inverted pleat, *two folds that face inwards and meet together*

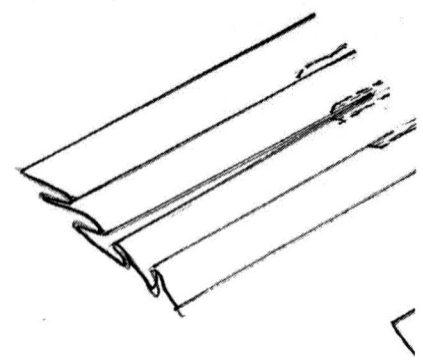

Invisible mending, *lengths of yarn are unravelled from within the seams and used to replace the pattern of the fabric where there is a hole. This requires considerable skill*

Jap silk, *the lightest weight and least expensive silk*

Jersey, *a knitted fabric in a variety of yarns*

Lurex, *a shimmering metallic thread used for embroidery or woven or knitted into fabric*

Lute binding, *a half inch straight binding used by tailors for a variety of purposes*

Mohair, *cloth made of the long hair of the Angora goat*

Moiré, *silk or synthetic fabric with a watered surface.*

Mull, *an inexpensive muslin like fabric used for pattern making*

Nap, *a woolly surface on the cloth, raised by a finishing process (as opposed to pile which is made in the weaving process.) A garment must be made with the nap brushing down otherwise the garment will pill*
Organdie, *a very fine and almost transparent, stiffened cotton*
Organza, *sheer fine silk or synthetic yarn which is naturally stiff*
Organzine, *a silk yarn of two or more threads thrown together with a slight twist*
Over sew, (overcasting) *to stitch over the edge of a seam to prevent fraying*
Pad stitching, *diagonal stitching used to attach the canvas to the under side of the fabric in tailored garments*

Pad stitching is usually used for the revers and the underside of the back collar

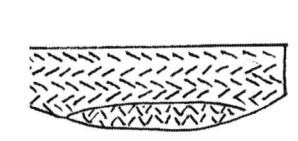

Petersham ribbon, *a stiffly-ribbed ribbon usually made of rayon or nylon*
Pile, *a covering of hair or yarn (ie velvet) which is constructed in the manufacture and usually processed to lay in one particular direction*
Pill, *rub up and become hairless*
Pinking scissors, *scissors that cut in a zig-zag to prevent fraying but definitely not used in couture dressmaking*

Pin tuck, *a very fine tuck of about 2mm is stitched close to the edge*
Pin stitch, *stitching very close to the edge*
Piping, *a piece of folded fabric, usually on the cross inserted between the edge of the fabric and the facing. Sometimes it has cord inserted into it*
Placket, *an opening with press fastener and hooks and eye fixing, used before the invention of zip fasteners. A seam, usually on the left hand side of the bodice, was left open. The top side was faced with a piece of crossway fabric and the under side was bound with a strip of fabric*
Piqué, *a ribbed cotton, used for crisp collars and cuffs*
Pongee, *a fine silk made from the cocoons of the wild silkworm, or a fine cotton— mostly used for linings*
Prick stitch, *a tiny hand stitch used to hold down the turnings*
Princess line, *a dress cut in panels from shoulder to hem and fitted at the waistline*
Raw silk, *a heavy slubbed silk, mostly in a natural shades of beige*
Run and fell, *a seam stitched with the top turning half the width of the bottom turning. Then the under turning is folded over and turned under before being hemmed or felled*

Rouleau, *a narrow crossway strip of fine fabric stitched and turned out to make a rope, often used to make button loops*

Ruching, *gathering up fabric on both sides to give a raised effect, often used for trimming*

Russian Braid, *a narrow braid with a rib down the centre*

Saddle stitch, *a bold even-running stitch, used for decorating*

Satin, *a shiny silk or rayon fabric*

Satin stitch, *often padded, stitches can vary in length but set close together alongside one another*

Selvedge, *the manufacturer's edge to the fabric. It is usually cut off or notched with scissors diagonally to remove any tightness*

Shantung, *a plain rough cloth of wild silk*

Shell stitch, *a narrow hem which has a tight vertical stitch over the top of the hem to draw it in at intervals, thus creating a shell like edging—*

Slip stitch, *stitching from the outside of the garment, slide the needle through the fold of the seam alternately on each side of the seam to attach them together.*

Slub silk, *pure silk with the slub joins showing prominently*

Spit! *take a long length of white cotton, chew it well in the mouth and use to remove blood, resulting from a pricked finger. Start from outside the stain, working to the centre. Repeat with fresh pieces of chewed cotton, until the stain has disappeared*

Sprat's head, *an embroidered shape that was put at the top of a pleat or opening to prevent it splitting out under pressure*

Stitch and turn out, *stitch the seams and turn to the other side, as when making a pillowcase.*

Sunray pleat, *a machine made pleat on to a circle, which has a corrugated appearance*

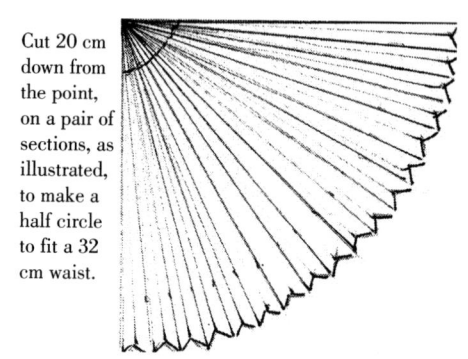

Cut 20 cm down from the point, on a pair of sections, as illustrated, to make a half circle to fit a 32 cm waist.

Taffeta, *a fine slightly stiff silk or synthetic fabric, with a slightly shiny appearance, the warp and the weft often woven in two different colours*

Tailors chalk, *a flat block of hard white chalk, 4cm square with sharp chiselled edges that draw fine lines*

Tailor tack, *tacking with a small stitch and using double thread, the outline of the pattern is marked on to both sides of the fabric together. The two pieces of fabric are pulled apart and the tacking thread cut through the middle, leaving whiskers of thread to mark the line on each side*

Thai silk, *brilliant coloured silk of the highest quality*

Thimble, *a necessary protection for the top of the finger of a dressmaker or tailor*

Toggle, *a lozenge shaped piece of wood, which is used to thread through a loop for fastening*

Toile, *a mock-up of the garment made of mull or in our case often lining, prepared for the first fitting. Or a mull pattern sold by the French couturiers to wholesalers for mass production*

Top stitch, *a decorative stitching on the top side of a seam*

Trace tack, *marking the line to be stitched with a tack, which crosses over at any junction to indicate an absolute position*

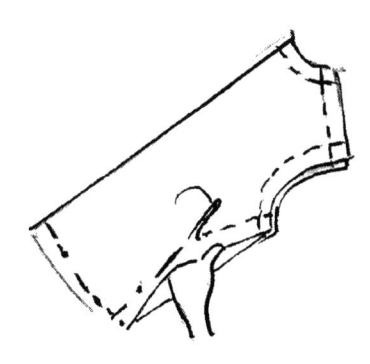

Tulle, *a delicate thin silk or nylon network fabric*

Ultrasuede, *a synthetic suede made from polyester and polyurethane, which is crease resistant and washable. It is not so robust as Alcantara, which is almost indestructible and of a heavier weight than ultrasuede*

Unbleached calico, *see 'calico'; the unbleached is used for covers and can be extremely thick and strong*

Voile, *a thin semi-transparent material*

Warp, *the threads stretched out lengthways in a loom to be crossed by the weft (or woof)*

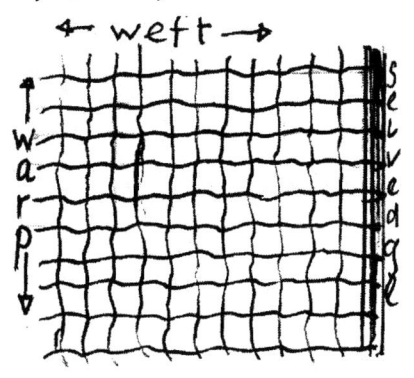

The horizontal threads are called WEFT & the lengthway threads are called the WARP

Vendeuse, *a French name for a fashion sales assistant*

Waspie, *a shape designed to give a woman a 'Wasp Waist'*

Wild silk, *or tusser, a fine silk from India*

Weft, *(or woof) is the thread that is on the shuttle and goes across the fabric*

Whip stitch, *a small overcasting stitch*

Worsted, *(Worstead, a village near Norwich) A fine, smooth, closely-woven woollen fabric, made from a yarn that has been spun out of long combed wool*

Yarn, *a spun thread used for knitting or weaving.*

Yoke, *the part of the garment that fits the shoulders or the hips*

Zip, *designed to replace the press fastener placket, it was originally made of metal and of a heavy construction. Now available in nylon construction in many weights*

**Inventory of Garments,
donated by Estelle Addington & Thelma Marks, of
D'Arcy & Rosamunde Ltd of Bedford, to the Cecil Higgins Art Gallery.
2001 — 2005**
*Those garments carrying the D'ARCY label, were all designed and made in
the D'Arcy & Rosamunde workroom, at number 42 Harpur Street, Bedford.*

1947   Designed by Thelma for herself, — a purple and turquoise striped taffeta strapless **Evening Gown**. The skirt is cut on the cross, so as to mitre at the front and back, where there is also a bustle . Crossway **Stole** to match. Worn over a stiff petticoat.

1952   D'ARCY strapless **Evening Gown** made of dark red and cream satin striped furnishing fabric. The stripes are pleated to produce a dark red bodice that accentuates the waist. The top of the bodice and the waist are cuffed with a matching red silk, which hangs in a sash at the back. Made for the window display of Elizabeth II coronation. (Worn over a stiff petticoat.)

1953   D'ARCY half circle chequered short **Evening Skirt**, with squares of gathered net and rose-patterned bronze and black Sekers brocade, worn with a separate long-sleeved velvet **Bodice**. Made from "cabbage" i.e. leftover fabric!

1954   D'ARCY Mix & Match orange course linen **Duster Coat** and matching **Dress**,
The dress shows the typical work that went into a D'Arcy dress. Note the drawn thread work through the front. The bodice is embroidered with the drawn threads and the design is highlighted with white beads. Most models of this calibre were sold, the most outstanding being of grey flannel with self-embroidery, high lighted with yellow beads that resembled mimosa— *Plus* **an Alternative Dress** of matching cotton lace, mounted on to cross-cut linen.   (3 items— I coat and 2 dresses)

1958   D'ARCY short strapless **Evening Gown**, made of silver grey, pure silk satin, embroidered in stripes with gold thread and coral silk in a rose design.
Plus pink tiered nylon **Slip**, worn under this dress.

1959   D'ARCY electric blue and black striped **Cotton Dress**, with full skirt and black shaped leather belt. Made of sail-cloth, it is typical of the summer dresses of the period. Worn over a full-tiered nylon slip.

1959   D'ARCY —full skirted tiered pink nylon **Slip** with a tightly fitting bodice, which was worn under the blue and black striped cotton dress, and others at the time.

1960   D'ARCY floral embroidered **Dress** of pure silk cream shantung. A simple, very low-necked dress, the neckline is held in place with elastic under the arms and around the back. It is banded under the bust with olive green silk.

1960 D'ARCY navy and white jacquard **Suit,** with a cropped jacket and wide-cuffed neckline, is made in an exclusive French fabric. The yarn content is unknown, as at that time it was not mandatory to say how to care for the garment or to identify the yarn content. *Needless to say, it would need to be dry-cleaned.*

1962 D'ARCY —long slinky **Evening Gown** of pink silk and silver lurex cloque fabric. It was worn with matching silk shoes. A glamorous range, of wired and boned corselets were stocked at the time. This dress was built on one of these, with a plunging neckline. Matching pink silk was used to edge the bra, in case it should show. It was considered a very daring dress at the time.

1963 D'ARCY cocktail **Gown** of turquoise silk cloque, diagonally checked with silver lurex. It is cut in a simple sheath with slits at the side and with a wide cuffed neckline.

1963 D'ARCY long **Evening Gown** made of heavily embossed and raised pure silk brocade, in shades of red and shocking pink. The detail is in the empire line bodice, which has a low neckline at the front but also a plunge neckline at the back, which is banded and knotted at the shoulder to keep it in place. The simple straight skirt has a fish-tail hem, which touches the floor at the back.

1964 D'ARCY dramatic full-length **Cloak** in purple velvet. It is worn over a matching ankle length sleeveless **Dress**, over an extravagant bishop sleeved **Blouse** of crisp heavy silk faille, in a purple and white design.

1965 D'ARCY simple full-length **Evening Gown** of sea green lace. This evening gown is a good example of many the evening and wedding dresses that were made to measure. The fabric was comparatively inexpensive, but the value was in the cut and fit. Once a customer was accustomed to this standard of fit, clothes irritated if they did not fit properly and so in this way we built up our regular clientele.

1968 An early import from Hong Kong, this full-length **Evening Gown** in turquoise wild silk, has a double lining to support the weight of the drop beads. It is beautifully made and retailed for around £40! That was an incredible price even at that time. It made us aware that we should be unable to compete in our workroom and sounded its death knell.

1968 D'ARCY simple sheath **Dress** made of a very expensive and beautiful fabric. The white woven wool has a machine-embroidered design all over it. This design was photographed and made a splendid background for our Autumn Show invitation.

1968   JEAN PATOU *ready-to-wear collection*, a red wool suiting **Dress and Jacket,** trimmed with white leather. Superbly made by Russian immigrant tailors, who reputably earned more than the principals of the company. When these tailors retired, there were no replacements and the company went out of business in the mid 1970s.

1968   JEAN PATOU *ready-to-wear collection,* another superbly made, sea-green **Dress** and matching full length **Coat,** trimmed with white leather.

Late 1960 Early 1970   A Collection of Children's clothes, designed and made for Johanna Marks
Central heating was by no means universal, so the weight and warmth of these dresses, which were worn with matching woollen tights should be noted.

1968   D'ARCY red and green tartan **Reversible Cape**, with its matching **Beret**.
And, to wear underneath, **a Pinafore Dress**, with matching skirt and bottle green bodice, worn over a white **Embroidered Blouse**.
Plus *alternative dress below.*

1968   D'ARCY bottle green woollen **Dress**, trimmed with white guipure lace to wear under cape. Note that it was lined with Viyella for warmth!

1968   D'ARCY green and blue long sleeved check wool Viyella **Dress**

1969   D'ARCY blue and cerise Austrian style **Dress**, lined with winceyette. Plus a matching short **Pinafore** that ties at the waist.

1970   D'ARCY blue and green herring bone wool **- Jacket, Trousers and Skirt**.
This outfit was made from a remnant and was a great favourite, as it mimicked the grown-up style of the time.

1970   D'ARCY printed cotton organdie **Party Dress**, with lace bib and puffed sleeves edged with lace.

1971   D'ARCY orange and white striped cotton **Dress**, trimmed with white lace.

1972   Pink check cotton gingham, made into a **Dress** by Johanna herself (aged 10)

Note that the woollen dresses needed to be dry cleaned, so that they were only worn for special occasions and were taken off on returning home. Pinafores were also worn when eating, so as not to stain them. This followed the pattern of life of earlier generations.

1972 TRICOSA of Paris green tweed jersey full length **Coat** and matching sheath **Dress** from the premier French knitwear company of the period. The 1972 catalogue shows other colours and styles available in this fabric.

1973 D'ARCY model **Dress** made of a fine wool challis fabric, printed in harlequin checks of pink, orange, mauve and grey. Note the couture attention to detail — each button and button hole is of a different colour, to match the corresponding check. *This fabric must be dry-cleaned.*

1974 MARIS of Germany. A Herring-bone fitted **Coat** with a beautiful and rare **Lynx collar**. This is another example of the mass-produced German tailoring, which emerged in the 1970s.

1975 RALPH of Munich. A classic **Coat** made of pebble dash beige and white tweed, ideal for racing and being neutral, it could be worn over practically anything.

1975 DOLORES — a very expensive hand-blocked Lynx **Hat**. No one then realized that the lynx faced extinction! Retail price originally £500,

1975 TRICOSA of Paris, a **Short Evening Gown** of gossamer fine-printed jersey, with shoe string straps and matching **Stole**— (and **Slip**)

1975 CAMP of Switzerland embroidered black jersey mounted onto Vilene to make a flared **Skirt** and **Bolero,** all edged with a wide embroidered design. It was worn with a black polo-necked sweater.

1975 CAMP of Switzerland produced this sporty **Trouser suit.** The trousers are made of tan wool jersey and the matching suede jerkin has knitted sleeves and collar. Comfortable to wear, it was an expensive item to service, as each time it was dry cleaned, it was very costly.

1975 ANNA ROOSE A brown woollen **Waistcoat Suit**, made by from the un-dyed wool of the Jacob sheep . The matching cream embroidered Mediaeval style waistcoat has a row of round silver buttons with loops fastening from neck to waist. It is worn with a cream pin-tucked fine wool **Blouse**, which has a ruffle neck and sleeves.
*Originally worn with a matching long cape, with a hood, which may be available later.

1976 D'ARCY long tiered patchwork **Evening Skirt** made of Marcel Boussac Cotton and banded at the hem with a black printed cotton.

1976 D'ARCY tiered long **Evening Skirt**, made of remnants of Chinese silk in ivory and pink and trimmed with brown velvet

1977 CHATEAU d'ESTE —**Dinner Gown** of fine Liberty wool in a beautiful paisley border design in shades of brown and pink. This was a great period when the cocktail dress disappeared for a while and graceful long gowns were worn.

1977 SUNFASHIONS from Hawaii, a cleverly sunray-pleated long **Evening Dress,** which would fit any size! They came in many design and colours and sold at £15.

1977 HAWAII matching **Bikini and Jacket** in a multi-coloured print of shocking pink, blue and green.

1978 LAURA APONTE, a sensual **Dress** in fine navy blue silky jersey from Rome, worn by Estelle. — It needs a tall elegant woman to wear it.

1978 TRICOSA of Paris, a blue princess line **Coat** made of Alcantara, which is washable, waterproof and almost indestructible. It is the first of the suede look fabrics, which resulted from a discovery in space travel. The felted fabric was made in a vacuum. Later there were many similar fabrics developed, which were less costly, but not so good as the original.

1981 ELISSA of Spain, a pale lemon knitted **Dress** with **Scarf**. For two or three years, these knitted dresses were an answer to many needs. Hand-loomed from a mixture of acrylic and polyamide, they were washable and easy to wear. They were available in many pretty colours and often only semi-fitting, so as to accommodate many sizes. It was sad when the market became saturated.

1982 PAREGGIO of Italy —An intricately pleated cream georgette **Dress** in a classic shirtwaist style, this is understated elegance at its best. These dresses were sold in a range of beautiful colours and styles, which were popular for weddings.

Plus Sundry items

1950s A red straw and velvet **Hat**, made with two matching **hat pins.**

1950s A caramel straw **Hat**, made with a matching **hat pin**

1958 6 short **Hooped waist slips**

1948 A "Waspy" worn by Thelma marks under the pinched waists of the New Look skirts and suits.

1953 Two boned **Corselets** made form oddments and used at D'Arcy & Rosamunde shows, before the correct fabrics were available.
Some Other Items

INDEX

Alterations 67
Alps 34
Alconbury 57
Admiral 36
Advertising design 51
Advertising agent 79
Age of Elegance 63
Amazons 71
America(n) 36,77,98
Andre Courreges 71
Anglia Television 80,83
Anglo Timber 53
Anthony Armstrong Jones 70
Animal Rights 34
Anne Crawford 52
Apprentice 45,48
Apprenticeship 18
Art of lettering 51
Ascot 36,37,63
Astrakhan 33
Atrima 28,29
Avenue Matignon 61
Balenciaga 62
Ball(s) 32
Balmain (Pierre) 60,61
Bangladesh 92
Bare midriff 65
Barbara Cartland 36
Barbara Hulanicki 69
Bargains 75,76
Barathea 29
Barrett Street 11
Bazaar 69
Beagleys 17
Bearskin 33
Betty Brierley 57
Beaver 33
Bedford 11,15,17,22,5571,86
Bedford Physical Training College 70
Bedfordshire Times 80
Biba 62,69
Blitz 12

Bodileys 25
Book-Keeping 20
Bournemouth 88
Boussac 29
Bride 39,40,42,43,45
Bride's father 41
Bride's mother 40,44
Bridesmaids 39
British Red Cross 86
Broadway 15
Bruton Street 63
Budget 97
Buckingham Palace 36
Burglary 99
Bush House 54
Caroline Bacon 7,102,103
Canada 31
Capital 19,20
Cardington hangars 80,83,102
Carnaby Street 69
Carrickmacross 44
Carven 60
Cecil Higgins Art Gallery 102, -103,104
Cedar House School 27
Claire Cobden 33
Chanel 60,85
Charing Cross Road 13
Charity Shops 34
Charter Window Display 73
Chef George 60,61,62
Chelsea 69
Cherry Marshall 14
Chiffon 46
Children 47
Chinese 87
Christmas 64, 76
Christian Dior 63
Christian faith 92
Civic Theatre 57
Cleveland Square 54
Claire 75
Coco Chanel 85

Cold Storage 33
Collection 28,102
Colton 86
Common market 83
Concourse d'Elegance 60
Convent 29
Corn Exchange 32,57
Cornwall 88
Corselette 27
County 20,21,35
Court gowns 31
Couture 51,60
Covent garden 39,55
Credit 21
Crimplene 76,94
Christian Dior 60
Crofton Rooms 56,57
Customers 35
Customs and Excise 28
Dame Alice Street 101
D'Arcy (model) 36,37,45, 62
D'Arcy & Rosamunde ,104, ----47,41,68,70,83,86,87,93,94,103
David Addington 67
David Marks 66, 57
Debenham and Freebody 50
Deborah Kerr 52
Designing 51
Diamanté 37
Dickens & Jones 14
Dior (Christian) 50,63,64,76
Display cards 52
Disposable society 91
Dorothy Butler 56
Draper's Record 88
Dubonnet 65
Dusseldorf 72
Easter Day 64 ,65
Easter weekend 99
Eastern Bloc 87
Eastern Electricity 22, 25,
Easy care 76,94
Ecclesiastes 101

Edwardian 40
Electricity 20
Elizabeth Arden 37,63
Embroidery 48
English 88
E.P.Rose and Sons 34
Ermine 31
Estelle 14,21,28,29,30,56,62,66, 67,68,75,97,98,101,103,107
Ethiopia 92
Ethnic fashions 95
Ettrick Napier Mathieson 21
Europe 87
Evening Gowns 52
Evening Standard 52
Farm 11,17,68
Fashion 14
Fashion jewellery 64
Fashion Show (s) 50,71,84
Father 11,17,19,21,22,25,42,68
Faubourge St Honoré 61
Fittings 18
Follies Bergere 61
Fox 33
Francis Madden 12
Frazers 15
Freedom from hunger 71
French 88,92
French modelling 51
Furrier 31,33
Guards 94
Gas Ring 18
German 88
Ginette Spanier 60
Givenchy 62
Gladys Clayton 15
Gloves 59,86
Golf umbrellas 43
Goldington Road 31
Goodwill 18
Goodyear airship 63
Grandmother 40
Grosvenor Street 28
Gruau 95
Guineas 24

Handbags 86
Hanwell 14,53,54
Hats 86,93
Hat shop 67
Hardy Amies 51
Hardy's Thornproof 24
Harris Tweed 49
Harpur Street 11
Harrods ('arrods) 34,35,39
Harwich 100
Hat(s) 25,58,59
Haute Couture 11
Herts & Beds Topic 83
High Street 19
Hippies 95
Hinchingbrooke 32,86
History of Costume 51, 71
Hockliffes 15
Holborn 53
Hook of Holland 100
Hong Kong 42, 86
Hotel Cité Bergere 60
Hucke 73
Interest 25
Investment 25
Irish Bride 42
Irons 18
Jack Freedman 28
Jacques Griffe 62
Jacques Heim 61,85
Jacqmar 28
Jean Patou 94
Jessie Jackson 15
Jewellery 86
Jo 75
John Lawrence 103
Joan Craddock 48,109
Joy Ricardo 27, 42
Kate Greenaway 95
Keith Joseph 89
Korea 87
Kimbolton Castle 34
Kings Cross 12
Kings Road 69
Knife sharpener 47

Lancaster Gate 11
Lady Diana Spencer 92
Lafega 16,23,24
Lagerfeld 85
Laura Ashley 95
Layered look 93
Leg of Mutton sleeve 40,41
Leopard 34
Liberty's 69,85
Life drawing 51
Lily Eayrs 30
Lloyds Bank 19
L' Officiel 65,94,95
Louise 75
London College of Fashion 11
London 11,17,34,38,49,55, 57,63, 64,67,70
Low pay 91
Lynx 34
Madame 21
Margaret 17,23
Ma Griffe 60
Marmot 34
Marriage 41
Marshall's of Cambridge 83
Mary Quant 62,68
Mass production 91
Matty 21,22,84
Midi 85
Mini skirt 69
Mink 31
Mini Brides 36,37
Miss Craig 66
Miss Faulkner 17,23,24,25,29, 38 58,66
Models 67
Mondi 73
Mondrian 72
Monica Wilkinson 63,66,75, 98, 108
Mother 19,23,30,46,66, 67,68
Morris Eight 59,60
Mrs.Allen..66
Mrs East 63

Mrs Christopher Soames 71
Mrs Dowler 46
Mrs Graham 37
Mrs May 16,18
Mrs Philcox 66
Mull 112
Munrospun 62
Musquash 33
Next to Nellie 18,45,47,48
New Look 50,51
Newsletter 74
Nissen hut 53
Norman Hartnell 63
Nur kostum 72
Nylon 94
Ocelet (paws) 34
Olympia 13
Opera 12,55
Oxford Circus 50
Paddington 11
Paris 35,60,64,79,83,95
Parachute 49
Pauline 28
Physiotherapist 93
Pictures 12
Pierre Balmain 60,61
Personnel managers 46
Police Station 21
Police 99,100,101
Polly Peck 69
Pony Skin 33
PR 12,79.80
Prince of Wales 92
Princess Alexandra 71, 72
Princess line 49
Princess Margaret 70
Profit 20
Queen 70
Queen Mother 70
Rabbit 34
Ralph of Munich 73
Rates 20
Ready-to-Wear 28
Rent(s) 20,99
Roger & Gallet 61

Ready-to-wear 63,64
Regency 16,18
Regency Terrace 31
Reputation 41
Rima 28,
Rogaire 85
Roger 75
Rosamunde 15
Sable 29,31
Sale 23, 76
Sari 46
Saturdays 41
Savile Row 17
Savoy Hotel 41
Scotland 88
Seal skin 33
Sea Island cotton 94
Second World War 11,49,65
Selfridges 49
Shakespeare 29
Shamrocks 44
Shift dresses 76
Sheepskin 33
Shoe(s) 25,59,86
Shophound 88
Shoplifting 76
Sports clothes 88,97
Siberia 31
Simon Massey 28
Singapore 87
Sister 23
Ski 24
Space Age 71
Spain 97
Special Constable 22
Spring Collection 28
Squirrel 32
Statistics 110
St. Cuthbert's Street 56
St. Martin's College of Art 13,55
St. Peter's Street 31
St. Paul's Church 40
St. Neots 12,21,56
Streaking 91
Stock 18

Stockings 58
Stocktaking 20
Storage Heater 21,24
Spring 1952 27
Swinging Sixties 69
Sylvia 17
Tailors 85
Tailoring 113
Trades Unions 87
Theatre 12
Thelma 30,44,48
Tights 58
Times newspaper 89
Tower Bridge 54
Tricosa 63,76,79,97
Trevor Fenwick 31,34
Trouser suit 87
Twenty-fifth 89
Union 91
Utility 16
Vendeuse 16
Victorian era 96
Vivienne Westwood 96
Vogue 60,88,95
Wanda 108
Wages 20,67
Wages Board 89
Wages Council 90
Wales 88
War Ag 11
Waspie 36
Weddings 39,40,41,43
Wedding gown 44,114
Welcome 83
Wellingborough 35
West End 14,55
Westminster Bank 19
Wholesale(r) 12,14,18
Wool 38
Woollen suiting 38
Worldwide Fund 34
Workroom 16,23,45
Worth 50
Yves St. Laurent 71
Zen 91
Zig-zag 67